CASH FL

10 steps to CREATING WEALTH IN ANY ...

Written by J. MASSEY,
"Investorpreneur and Problem-Solver"

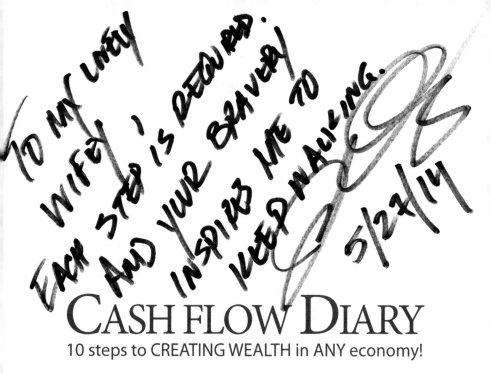

To my lucky
wifey!
Each step is required.
And your bravery
inspires me to
keep making.
5/27/14

CASH FLOW DIARY
10 steps to CREATING WEALTH in ANY economy!

Written by J. MASSEY,
"Investorpreneur and Problem-Solver"

Published by West Egg Enterprises, Inc.
27472 Portola Ranch, #205-321
Foothill Ranch, Calif. 92610

Book design by Dori Beeler
Cover design by Dori Beeler
Edited by Sandra Rea, Full Circle Media & Author Promotions

For information regarding special discounts for bulk purchases, please send your request to info@cashflowdiary.com or call 800-689-1764.

ISBN:978-0-9915903-0-8

DEDICATION

For my four beautiful children. I love you and hope this book gives you a glimpse into your father's mind. Scary, huh? Now you can understand what I mean when I say that you need to come up with a product or service to create the value you then will sell to buy that new video game or doodad you just asked me to buy for you. I am proud of all of you for being independent spirits.

For my wife, Popi. You are my inspiration, my motivation, and the love of my life. Thank you for supporting me through the years. Thank you for being my "umbrella... eh, eh, eh, eh"!!

ACKNOWLEDGEMENTS

It takes a team of talented individuals to build true success in any realm. On my path this is certainly the case, and I want to thank each and every team member for his/her dedication and hard work. I ask a lot sometimes, and I know it. Thank you for hanging in there with me and for continuing to support our shared vision. I look forward to working with you far into the future. Thank you, KimBerly Keyton, VP Operations; Jennifer Cayton, CFO; Jake Bongiovanni, Christina Haftman, Sandra Rea-McGinty, Andrée Caldwell and Linda Solis.

I thank my mentors along the way, too. I have worked with some amazing people and I have learned from them all. I have also learned from individuals I've never met who have written books that I can highly recommend. In no particular order I want to thank Robert and Kim Kiyosaki, Stephen Gregg, Eric Lofholm, Chris Jennings, Matt Sorenson, Jim Allfrey, Bob Snyder, Mark Kohler, Dr. Joyce Meyers, Blair Singer, Michael Gerber, Jeff Olson, Stephen Covey, Russell Grey, Robert Helms, Ken McElroy, Jason Stephens, Brian Bailey, Jeff Hickman, Danny Saltz, Anthony Robbins, Chris Wilson, Dani Johnson, Kim Klaver, Tim Sales, John Maxwell, Malcolm Gladwell, Timothy Ferris, Dale Carnegie, George S. Clayson, Dr. David J. Schwartz, Marcus Buckingham, Dr. Gary Chapman, Brendon Burchard, Gary Vaynerchuk, Simon Sinek, Randy Kepford, Erol Woods, Wallace D. Wattles, Chris Albin, Jeff Armstrong, Sean Breshears, Mike Hinsvark, James Keys, Nancy Dana, Del Hargis, John Dessauer, Adrian Cobbarubias, James Leis,

John Varughese, The Honorable Judge Larry Potter, Mayor A.C. Wharton, Curtis Braden, Noah Withington, Chris Weiler, Jenni Nering, Rosie and Robert Penn, Robert Kaempen, Patrick Sharples, Dustin Sichon, Jeff Smyth, Matt Theriault, Malcolm Turner and Dave Zook, Hugh Borthwick. Please forgive me if I left any names out!

I also thank those who have passed from this world whose advice and guidance continues to be invaluable: Chad Wade, Justin Yates, Zig Ziglar, Jim Rohn, Frank Alcorn and Dan Reese. You are truly missed.

To my mother and father, thank you for encouraging me to follow my dreams. And to all of the mothers, fathers, sons and daughters who are still willing to fight for their dreams. To the servicemen and women who still protect our ability to dream.

Finally, thank you, God, Jesus and the Holy Father who help me keep it all together every day of my life. I am grateful.

TABLE OF CONTENTS

Introduction
  What TIME is it?   p 1

STEP ONE:
  Get Started!   p 9

STEP TWO:
  No Money? No Problem. Your Fears; Your Problem!   p 59

STEP THREE:
  Don't Lose Money.   p 107

STEP FOUR:
  Stop Listening to Lies!   p 127

STEP FIVE:
  Train Your Brain. Mindset Matters.   p 141

STEP SIX:
  Develop a Team Game Plan.   p 191

STEP SEVEN:
  Don't Just Break Even…Consider the Whole Package.   p 217

STEP EIGHT:
  Think Outside the "Box."   p 229

STEP NINE:
  Think Creatively!   p 255

STEP TEN:
  Be Courageous.   p 285

CONCLUSION   p 295

FOREWARD

By Robert Helms and Russell Gray, Hosts of
The Real Estate Guys™ Radio Show

Having read a lot of books, we know that not everyone reads the foreward, so thanks for taking time to read this one. We're honored to have written it and are here to tell you that you're in for a treat.

However, it's not like the world needed another book on real estate investing. So what's special about this one and why is it worthy of your time? Great question!

In these pages you will meet the amazing J. Massey. We'll let you discover for yourself what makes J. so amazing. If you're lucky and resourceful, you'll find a way to get into a relationship with him. We try to do our part to share J. with the world because of how much we've enjoyed our relationship with him and his lovely wife Popi. They're great people; their passion for life and for helping others is contagious. You can't help but be excited whenever you're around them.

As you read this book, you'll learn real estate investing through J.'s real-life experiences. This is important because it's J. and Popi's lives that make the lessons powerful. J.'s long arms will literally reach out of the pages to shake your shoulders and enthusiastically proclaim, "You CAN do it!" And only someone who's lived J.'s life can say that with credibility.

Ultimately, success comes down to taking effective action. Knowing what to do isn't enough. Being excited isn't enough. Having all the right advisors and providential opportunities isn't enough.

Until you BELIEVE you can, you'll hesitate. You'll sit out or hold back when you should charge.

So while J. is a great investor… savvy, smart, disciplined, hardworking, intelligent, creative… more than anything he's credible. He isn't regurgitating theories he heard in some seminar. He's sharing his own personal real-life wisdom earned in the school of hard knocks. And if he seems a little rah-rah, just remember where he came from.

J. knows the real secret to success isn't a formula, technique or strategy. It's an attitude and a mindset. In these pages he pours himself out to help ignite that winning attitude in you. He fuels the fire with practical knowledge gleaned from real-world deal making. But without that spark of belief, all the knowledge in the world can't help you.

Get ready for a fun ride into the heart and mind of J. Massey as he shares with you his proven system for creating wealth in any economy… to help you, no matter where you are right now.

Robert Helms and Russell Gray
Hosts, The Real Estate Guys™ Radio Show

INTRODUCTION

Right now, this very minute, I ask you…

What TIME is it?

I don't know what you just said, but in case you don't know, it's NOW o'clock! If you want to change things in your life you need to take action now. It's an adage that I live by and that my team lives by, so we do in fact practice what I've been teaching for years. We embrace taking immediate action at the Speed of Instruction™.

I could have given this book a different title, like Just Do It or What Are You Waiting For?! or Take Action and Don't Look Back because DOING "IT" is one of the main messages in this book. I want you to learn and then act quickly on that information. Then repeat time and time again until you're so good at what you do as a real estate investor that it's like tying your shoes! I want you to throw out old ideas that tell you to move slowly or that you need to handle every aspect of a deal. It's just not true.

1

I wrote this book to give you the tools and understanding of real estate investing to get you to move into action quickly and then keep moving. I want to hear from you not long from today (also known as now o'clock) telling me how well you're doing as a real estate investor and what tactics you are using in your business. Find me through my website at www. CashflowDiary.com.

On the other hand, if you are 100% satisfied with your life and finances, if you don't want to learn how to create tangible cash flow into your life that would allow you to improve the quality of not just your life but all the lives around you, if you like working a 9-to-5 job where you are not the boss, if you think you can find what this book teaches in some seminar or educational environment, I invite you to close the book now. This book is not for you. If, however, you want to learn by example about how I went from being homeless to homeowner and then a successful real estate investor who owns, at the time of this writing, more than 380 units of property in just a few short years, then keep reading. If you do, you'll learn how my doing 11 transactions in a week early on in my real estate investing career put me on the path I continue on today. If you like the idea of learning how I did that and how you can, too, you will find this a very helpful book indeed.

I wrote this book to help YOU do exactly what I did in real estate. Unlike some books we've all read that leave out the real action steps it takes to become successful as a real estate investor, I'm giving you the whole enchilada. I am

not intentionally leaving anything out. I truly want you to be more successful than I am, because there is plenty of room in the market for more people like me… and like you. If I could move through what I did in life to achieve what I have in just five years, so can you. But it's not magic. I have no magic wand and this is not a magical book of spells and incantations. Just by reading this you aren't suddenly going to have the ability to transform your life. It takes work. In short, it takes committed action. You get to choose to learn new skills and add to those you already have. You get to become a communicator, someone who is comfortable in sharing his/her vision with strangers. This is called developing "interpersonal skills" and you lean on them in all you do to improve the quality of your life and the size of your bank account if that is your true goal. In fact, I'll go out on a limb here and tell you that even if you don't become a real estate investor, this book will change and improve the way you view things in your life, in general. That is my intent. I want you to start looking at things… everything… in a different light. You have more power to control your destiny than you might think. How do I know? Because it is a truth that was revealed to me over the past few years. I'm living my dream.

Let me back up. I'll take you back to my 9-to-5 days. Don't think I'm bashing those who truly like being an employee. I'm not. Employee types are needed, too. It's just that I'm not one of them. If you like being employed, you too might want to close the book right about now. (Or keep reading and maybe I can open your mind to a new way of thinking.)

I worked for plenty of bosses in different companies. I gave it a shot! However, I was not satisfied working for other people. I asked too many questions (something I heard from my bosses a lot). I didn't get a lot of answers, which didn't make much sense to me. I was told often to "stop making waves" and to do "the job" like everyone else because that's the way it's supposed to be done. I'm glad I didn't listen. If I remained in those positions listening to the "bosses" about how to conduct my life, I wouldn't be here today writing this book and sharing with you all I have learned. I might still be struggling along, trying to make ends meet, deciding which bills I would pay this month and watching my credit score dip lower and lower. Today I don't care about my credit score (at least not the credit you think is credit). I don't have to! As a real estate investor who doesn't use his own cash or credit to buy, sell, or own properties, I don't have to care. My credit score doesn't matter. I'm sure one day my score will be top notch again, but I am also certain that I won't ever have to worry about it again. Why? I developed new skills and a new way of operating in my life.

You might be thinking, "Yes, J., but that's YOU. I can't do what you did. I have a family to take care of and lots of mouths to feed. How can I possibly stop what I'm doing and do something different?"

I assure you that I have several mouths to feed and they like food. (I know because I see it disappear from the fridge pretty quickly!) I have a great family that includes at the time of this writing four children ranging in age from toddler to full-blown

4

teen. My wife is and has always been very supportive of my goals and of me. She has been a part of my journey and she continues to be part of my success. She is intelligent, I look to her for input and we are a team. She is part of my company's team, too. So I don't buy the ol' "but I have a family" excuse for not learning a new way to bring money into the fold. There aren't many excuses I will buy. But don't misunderstand me. I am NOT telling you to quit your job… yet. I am saying that you can change your mindset and then your life. I am saying that if you take action steps to make this change, you can have it. However, it is your choice. Whether you change your life or not doesn't impact me; it impacts you and your loved ones. In fact, if you think about it, change in your life impacts your relatives who aren't even born yet. It can impact people you will never meet. What do I mean? Easy…

Through my efforts as an active real estate investor I help families I will never meet get into clean, safe, affordable housing. I make improvements to residences and apartment buildings that raise the quality of life for these families. It makes me feel good to know that I am literally helping people, and I couldn't do that if I hadn't become an active real estate investor. (Maybe I should really say "hyperactive.") As a problem solver in real estate, I learned to look at things with a much broader scope than some other investors so I can make these improvements. It is not the almighty dollar that I seek in what I do. It is my goal to leave a legacy that helps improve not just my children's lives and not just my wife's life, but also to positively affect as many people's lives as I possibly can. You may think it's a lofty goal, but it's not. No goal is too big.

We'll cover that in this book along with a lot of other positive ways to look at life and at real estate investing.

I aim to give you the basic tools to put to use immediately in the world to begin to affect true change in your life. I want you to implement what you learn at the Speed of Instruction. Learn it and use it right now, because you know what time it is... That's right. It's NOW o'clock!

Feel free to share the ideas presented in this book far and wide. Don't be secretive about the information. It is meant to be shared. In fact, once you have entered your journey into the brave new world of real estate investing, I want to hear from you. Email me from inside my website at www.CashflowDiary. com. I want to hear about your successes and your mistakes. Believe me... you will make plenty. Just wait till you read about a few of mine! For example, I'll tell you about my entry into real estate investing, the good and the bad. I'll tell you about how I did ELEVEN deals in a week when I was first wholesaling. And I'll tell you about a magnificent series of mistakes in what I like to call my experience with Fix 'n' Flip Gone Wild or my Fix 'n' Flop! I'll even tell you about how I got out of a burning building alive. (Okay, I wasn't in the building at the time it was in flames nor was anyone else, but it could have ended my life as a real estate investor had I let it.)

Why am I sharing these personal stories with you? I address mistakes and how beneficial they are to show you that you shouldn't let the FEAR of making mistakes or even actual burning buildings keep you from continuing on your path.

6

I also want you to understand quite clearly that you MUST make mistakes to be a success. Maybe you've heard quotes like that and have dismissed them or don't believe them. You consider it hype when someone tells you that the way to success is through failure. Maybe you feel like these statements could never apply to you and that you could never create the wealth that these "quote makers" have. Or maybe you believe that you can come out of the chute, not make any mistakes because you read this book and other books, and you're ready to make your millions in real estate now. Good luck on that.

I'm not here to hound you into believing that mistakes are going to happen, but I am telling you without a shadow of a doubt that they are necessary to the process of success. Don't believe me yet? Let me ask you how you learned whatever it is that you are an expert in right now. Did your current skill set come suddenly after reading a book or even a whole library of books? Was it spontaneous learning? Spontaneous wisdom? Or did you learn and then make mistakes, adjust your thinking, re-learn the skills, take action steps, apply what you know works, make more mistakes and then adjust again until you knew what you were doing fully? I'm guessing the latter. We learn by mistake. It is how our brains are designed. There is a progression toward success in anything and it involves how we apply learned knowledge. First we learn. Then we head out into the world to apply that knowledge. Until we've put into action what we have learned, we won't be able to accomplish our set goal. We won't likely do "it" right the first or maybe the second or third times, but eventually and with

7

plenty of practice we get good at applying the knowledge. In real estate our first deals are for experience; later deals are for profit. Through our mistakes we gain wisdom. Then we can teach others to avoid the mistakes we made to create a faster path to success.

You can argue with me, but this is a TRUTH. It's tough to argue truth. However, if you can give me an example of something you learned in which you never made a mistake in order to get a whole lot better at "it" I invite you to share your tale with me. All I know is that in real estate I made mistakes. Big ones. I learned from each and every mistake I made, too. That's how I can write these words you are reading now. I have a lot of experience as a real estate investor. Had I been worried about making mistakes I wouldn't have entered this arena. I wouldn't have the contacts or the ability to change lives as I do now. I am now thankful for the wisdom my mistakes have produced! I want you to be thankful for yours and learn from them. Apply all the new bits of knowledge you gain from them, and you will be where I am now. I'm waiting for you. Get ready to learn and apply this knowledge at the Speed of Instruction! Ready, set... let's get started.

STEP ONE:

Get Started!

"It is impossible to live without failing at something unless you live so cautiously that you might as well not have lived at all. In which case you have failed by default." J.K. Rowling

The only way I know how to show you how to get started as a real estate investor is to share my story with you about how I got started. But before I share my journey with you, let's cover some things you'll want to do to help your mind shift into a new way of thinking and being.

The first actual step to becoming a real estate investor is to start thinking like one! Believe that you can achieve a new way of life. Believe that you CAN develop a new set of skills that will change your life and the lives of those you love. This is not happy talk. I'm not blowing smoke up your skirt. It is truth. So how do you make this shift? Start by talking to people who make their living as real estate investors, think

9

about your goals in real estate and then take action. Educate yourself by reading books about real estate investing and building a business. You can find a few to start with on my website at www.CashflowDiary.com. I add books every month or so that I've read and that offer excellent guidance. Some might surprise you, but that's okay. Read them anyway. Many of the books are about aspects of entrepreneurialism. If you're going to be a real estate investor, you are going to have to be entrepreneurial-minded. Another thing you can do to shift your mindset is to attend classes on real estate investing that are taught by people who are successful as investors. Find yourself a good mentor, too. Learn all you can so you can be more prepared for the life you want. Expand your "financial intelligence"!

Financial intelligence starts in the home.

Every day, my family practices financial education in our home. By the time my kids are in elementary school, they have a good base of understanding about money. We don't just give our children money to buy whatever they want. If we did, what would we be doing for our children? (Aside from keeping them quiet temporarily… until they decide they want the next "thing" on their wish list.) We practice in the home what I teach outside the home. That's right! I want my kids to have a level of financial intelligence that the average person simply doesn't possess. Who else is going to teach them if not me? I want them to know that if they truly want something that they can have it. And that's exactly what I tell them.

When one of my children comes to me and says, "Daddy, I want a new [fill in the blank]," my response is always the same. I say, "That's wonderful, Honey. You can have it, but first you will need to create a product or service that you can sell to earn the money to buy it." What's really cool is that is exactly what my oldest daughter does. At 16 years of age, she gets it! She creates crocheted pieces to sell online, and she earns her own money to spend on things she wants. We have great conversations about business, life and money. I'm proud of her for taking her own path. It will lead her to greater and greater successes in life. What parent wouldn't want that for their child? I am one proud papa! Not just that, but my daughter also plays and teaches the Cashflow 101 game to her peers so they might learn about handling money and making investments. (We'll get to the importance of playing the Cashflow game a little later. That's a promise, and I always keep my promises.)

Back to financial intelligence.

Can you imagine what the world would be like if everyone from an early age would be indoctrinated into the understanding that you can have anything you want if you can develop a product or service and then learn to sell it? What if we looked at the world as problems looking for solutions and then provide those solutions? Systems are developed from providing solutions. I provide solutions. And that's what I'm trying to tell you to do. That's one reason I wrote this book.

People have been asking me to write a book for a couple of years. Okay, okay. I'm doing it! I had to first be open to the IDEA of writing a book. Then I had to educate myself on the process. But I found that, just like in real estate investing, I couldn't expect to just dip my toes into the water to get the book done. I had to jump into the pool wholeheartedly, cannonball-style! I'm happy to report that it was way more fun than I thought it would be and a lot less scary. In fact, you can count on me writing more books in the future. I can't wait!

It is my intent with this book to get you beyond your feelings of overwhelm about jumping into the great, big pool of real estate investing to where you actually have fun investing. If you are anything like me, you're going to love being a real estate investor. I know you're interested or you wouldn't have gotten this far in the book. To get you to consider the possibilities and to bring you to a point where you can SEE yourself as a real estate investor I have to share my story without leaving anything out. That way, you will understand that I am more like you than you might think and that if I can be successful as a real estate investor, you can do really well as a real estate investor, too. You just have to want it enough to work for it… to take action steps, one after the other. And you have to be willing to make mistakes and move forward anyway. Mistakes aren't going to kill you; in fact, they might just be wonderful things! I've made mistakes and some of them ended up leading me to excellent new relationships in business and investing. I'll share those with you, too. For now, I want you to know that all things truly are possible if only you believe. Easy for me to say? Not really. To get to this

mindset I first had to reach bottom. Hang on, hang on. We'll get there. I'm not done with this part yet.

What I know can make you a million dollars.

My intent in this book is specific. I am not just going to give you the fish; I am teaching you instead how to fish! My goal is to provide you with fish for generations. I want you to learn TO DO and then teach your children to do. I want you to pass everything I tell you in this book and in my program (videos, podcasts, manuals and everything else you can find on my site) down to younger generations. I want you to share with your children and grandchildren the lessons I learned along the way, what I did and how I did it, so you and future generations can do it, too.

Don't think for a minute I'm being grandiose here. What I've done is not magic. It's simply DOING IT that gets you where I am today. If you're feeling good, you do it. If you're feeling ill, you do it. No matter what's going on with you personally, you do it. In that way, you gain experience and then success.

There is no room for fear.

People are funny creatures. We let fear stop us from doing what we want to do in our hearts. We let other people tell us we can't [whatever]. We listen to them, and we listen to the negative self-talk that rattles around our minds that tells us the same. The truth is that fear can't stop you. It's how you react to your fear that matters. If you didn't experience fear from time to time, you'd be a robot or dead. You're not a robot or dead, are you? I didn't think so. That means you can manage your emotions and manage your response to fear.

You think I don't experience fear? I do, but I go ahead and do what needs to be done anyway. Even if I don't know every part of a deal or how to do a specific task involved, that doesn't stop me from doing the deal. If I had let fear stop me, I wouldn't be writing these words today. I wouldn't be steadily working toward my goal of owning 1,000 units of residential real estate (I'm about half way there!) and 1,000,000 square feet of commercial space. No, there were no typos in any if those numbers and I approve this message.

Now that you're going to change your thinking to accept the success you will allow yourself to achieve as a real estate investor, and now that you understand you will need to change your response to fear, we can move on. That is if you promise me right now that you will read books written by the action-steppers of the world to help motivate you! Again, a great starting point is the books I've read and have put up on my site at www.CashflowDiary.com. I can see you shaking your head up and down, so okay. Moving on, if you want to join me in my success, here are your next first steps on your path:

1) Create a Vision Book (much better than a bulky vision board)
2) Take the steps I share with you

3) Gather a strong team as you build your portfolio

4) Don't worry so much

Too simple? You are correct, because becoming a successful real estate investor isn't just that simple. You will find challenges in each of these "simple" steps. Before we move on, this would be a good place for you to grab a cup of coffee or hot tea. In fact, head out to a local Starbucks. Maybe you'll see me there with my iPad and phone. Maybe you'll see me there playing a rousing round of the Cashflow 101 game. After all, Starbucks is where I spend a lot of my time! You never know whom you will meet at Starbucks. For example, while I was in Memphis a few years back, one of my investors was sitting at Starbucks. A guy sat next to her and she started telling him about everything I do in real estate. He was really interested, but beyond that it ended up that he is a trainer and has ties to professional athletes. He was involved in a cool basketball camp for kids that also offers education. We chatted not too long after and I asked if I could do a financial literacy program at the next camp, since he had invited me. I love basketball, and I was a basketball player in my youth, so I could relate to the kids. Now I'm involved in a big way in these camps. All from a conversation that was struck up between two people at Starbucks. I love that kind of stuff!

Regardless of where you choose to read this book, get comfy. You might be a little blown away. It's best that you're sitting down as I tell you about how I literally went from homeless to homeowner and then real estate investor in a matter of weeks after my primary residence was foreclosed. You heard me correctly. I became a squatter in that residence and then turned everything around in a "short" period of time. I haven't stopped since, and I continue to have the same level of passion about real estate investing. What's changed is the size of the deals and what the deals continue to bring to my life. I won't share with you the size of my portfolio or the numbers in my bank account, but if you want to add a lot more zeros and commas to yours, keep reading. (Got your attention, huh?)

A glimpse of my life…

Today, I am the CEO of my company, West Egg Enterprises, Inc. Even with that title, I wear a few different hats and I do whatever tasks need to be done, so I'm not so sure about the title. I make decisions in landlord duties. My team and I raise private capital. As the face of the company, it's up to me to make sure people understand who we are and what we are aiming to achieve, which is to help more people in a lot of different ways. That's part of what this book is about. It helps in exposure for the company, so I can help more people. That's what my videos, podcasts, website, social media, coaching and Cashflow Creation System programs are all about. The way I see it, if I could go from homeless to homeowner (think rental property, because I still enjoy the convenience of renting) and maybe if I share my story with others, then they will be able to accomplish what I have. But my success didn't happen all at once. It took steps.

Let's roll back the calendar to 2006, the beginning of a two-

year personal journey that would change my life. At that time I was a financial planner, and I wasn't happy in that role. In 2005, my wife Popi was pregnant with what would have been our first child together. We were happy about the baby, but then she experienced a miscarriage. It was a devastating blow, but together we worked through the emotions and chose to keep moving forward. At the beginning of 2006, we bought our first condo. It was small, just over 1,200 square feet, and we paid $350,000 for it. Not bad, right? (Did you spill your coffee as you read that number?) Think again. Later I "sold" it for much less in the form of a foreclosure auction. Welcome to squatter-hood! Yes, I'm allowed to make up words now. Anyway, what can I say? I hadn't learned the ropes as a real estate investor yet. There were a lot of options and opportunities that were open to me, but I didn't understand that yet. Instead, I was knee deep in the emotionality of everything. But I digress...

Popi became pregnant again and, yes, that was my fault. Thank you very much. Because of our previous experience, we were cautiously optimistic. Unfortunately, as the pregnancy progressed my wife became very ill. It took us a little while to figure out what was going on. She almost died three times. I'm not sure that one is ever prepared for such events, but we prayed a lot and we got through the worst parts of the experience together. Popi was diagnosed with a condition called hyperemesis gravidarum; a rare complication of pregnancy characterized by intractable nausea, vomiting and dehydration that only 0.5% to 2% of pregnant women experience. Popi's case was severe, which meant she was in

17

fear of developing ketosis and malnutrition. In the simplest
of terms, the condition meant that she couldn't take in the
nutrition her body needed during her pregnancy. Even
holding bread and water down was a trick until the doctors
figured out what was wrong. Popi was placed on bed rest
much of the time. I needed to be with her and to help take care
of her, but I was working a lot of hours at the time, so I had a
major life decision to make.

I realized right away that I couldn't work so much and still
be there for my wife. The last I checked, it is impossible to
physically be in two places at once. This set a lot of dominoes
in motion. I couldn't focus on my job nor make good financial
planning decisions when I was under this level of duress
personally. I had to be home a lot and wasn't making much
money. That's when I started selling personal possessions on
eBay. This is how I tried to control my situation… selling items
from my wife's bedside in the hospital! I know it sounds a
little insane, but it's what I knew how to do at the time.

For example, when Comp USA was closing I could buy items
for pennies on the dollar to flip at a good profit. I found
DSL modems and bought all I found on the store shelves to
resell on eBay. I got them at $18 per unit and sold them for
$49.99 plus shipping and handling. From there I expanded to
clothing and other personal items. I literally went through our
closets and garage. I remember the panic feeling of digging
through things to find items to sell. (Right now, I guarantee
you that you have about $3,000 in merchandise you don't
need and can sell on Ebay if you really want to!) I also used

Liquidation.com and other bulk-buy wholesaler sites where I could find reasonably priced items to resell at a profit. At the time, I saw no other way to make money and still be at my wife's side. I would be the best eBay seller I could be and ride out this personal storm! It wasn't working as well as I needed it to, however, and we found ourselves falling further and further behind in our bills. We couldn't afford to pay all of the mortgage each month either, and this was before the loan-mod fad had kicked into high gear. We were moving toward 2007, a fateful year.

About this time a friend of mine told me that I needed to become a real estate investor. I looked at him like he was from another planet. My credit score was around the upper 300s. (Please note the word "upper." I'm trying to make it sound better!) How in the heck would I become a real estate investor? I didn't realize it at the time, but my friend got me to thinking. He had shown me a path. He had planted a seed. I didn't know it at the time, but I had taken my first steps. (Remember how I told you that changing your thinking is the very first thing you must do before becoming a real estate investor? It's true. I've lived it.) However, I was so stressed out with my personal issues that I didn't allow myself to think too much about it at that moment. (It was better to delay, right? Uh, wrong.) I decided instead that I needed to detox from what was going on in my life. I headed out to play volleyball.

I didn't play a lot of volleyball. My game is basketball, but playing volleyball was a great stress reducer for me. However, on this particular day it would be a life changer. At some point

19

during the game, I launched myself into the air to spike the ball. It felt great… until I came down and landed on another player, puncturing my lung and causing me a lot of pain. My attempt to reduce stress ended up adding more stress to my life than I could imagine. It was certain that my wife wouldn't be alone now. So there we were… both of us incapacitated and on bed rest with zero income. Ain't life grand? There was no way I could keep eBaying either; it's a lot of effort and not enough return! I guarantee that I couldn't move far enough from the bed to dig through closets. I couldn't walk very far at all. I couldn't do my work in financial planning, and I wasn't yet a real estate investor. Life was looking mighty grim, but we held on by the skin of our collective teeth till 2008.

Oh, what a year!

On February 13, 2008, our primary residence went to auction. Yes, I, J. Massey was foreclosed on. I know… ironic, huh? But it was a push point that would finally shove me into action. My family and I squatted in this bank-owned property for months. However, just 12 days after the bank took possession of our home I started learning live in the classroom setting about buying and selling real estate. Four months later my wife and I did our first transaction, which showed me that I really could do this thing. I could actually be a real estate investor, and a darned good one at that!

In short order, I kept learning and I kept buying, flipping and wholesaling/rehabbing properties. One property at a time, I

put into practice what I learned in my real estate studies until one day when I started buying apartment buildings! I now own hundreds of units across many states, including but not limited to Illinois, Indiana, Tennessee, Georgia and California. I'm working on deals in Colorado. There are great deals across our nation, so why not? Just recently, I closed a deal on a 182-unit property in Tennessee and I am simultaneously working on an international deal in Belize. I also just closed on a commercial building in Colorado. This space was formerly a bakery, but I have lots of plans for it that will create more revenue and help the residents who live near the space! I have a vision to build a massive portfolio primarily in the affordable housing space, just as my company's mission statement promises. It is not enough for me to simply provide for my family and keep food in their mouths. I wouldn't keep doing what I do in real estate if I didn't think I could help a lot of other people and help them be able to afford to put food in their families' mouths. Providing a better quality of life by creating clean, safe, affordable housing is a driving force for me and my team.

Working vs. investing as a way to put food on the table.

We all have to figure out a way to eat and to feed our families. It is a tangible experience. We are used to working X number of hours for X dollars in pay and then converting it to money in the bank to use for food and other essentials. Working like this is an active sport. We are "actively working." I didn't ever find this appealing. I wanted PASSIVE income. I didn't want to work in an office for a boss, but I had bills to pay and, like so many of us, before I became a real estate investor I traded my time (about nine or ten hours a day of it) for a paycheck. That meant I spent very little "off" time with my wife and kids. I happen to enjoy time with my wife and kids. Something had to change. It would be me. I had to shift my mindset from being an "employee" to an entrepreneur and investor. It took me some time to adjust and it will take you some time to adjust, so don't quit your day job yet, as they say.

My days as a company man...

I've had jobs as a "company man" and I can tell you that my bosses didn't care for my ideas. They didn't want me to do things my way and I usually couldn't understand WHY they did things the way they did. In one corporate job, I held the title of a customer service underwriter. I produced more than the other people on my team. I did things my way, but to be fair I also considered how other people did the job. My way happened to work best for me. I was a very high producer for the company, and though I wasn't happy with how things worked at that company I signed up for the job. I would have to accept the ways in which the company functioned. So I did, and I stuck with it... until one day.

The last straw with that particular company came on a typical day when the head honcho pulled me aside to chat with me about my future with the company. I was known for speaking my mind. This "boss lady" knew I wanted to go into sales

(the company offered a sales position) and she said I couldn't because I hadn't been with the company and/or at my job for three years. I stared at her. I'm pretty sure she could see what I was thinking. The eyebrows probably gave me away. What did that have to do with my abilities? I remember leaving her office disgruntled. Then I learned about a sales contest the company was hosting. Had it not been for the three-year rule that was holding me back from a sales position I wouldn't have been interested in participating in the contest, but there it was… a challenge. (I love a challenge!) So, I gathered my sales team. It was the last day of the contest. As the customer service underwriter, I taught my team a single technique that I used effectively and that's all it took. We did it! We won the sales contest in a single day. Yes… ONE DAY. I thought that by proving my abilities in sales that I would be allowed to go into sales training. I was mistaken. There would be no sales position for me. I ended up finding an opportunity to be a financial planner and would eventually learn how to be a good sales person on my own. I didn't really need that sales course after all; I needed a better one.

Sales are part of everything we do. Whether on the job, in everyday life or as a real estate investor, we are all sales people. Think about it. You have to sell yourself in all areas of your life. You must negotiate terms and make deals. I don't care if you are dealing with your children, your kids' schools or the car salesman down the road, the same skills apply. I guarantee that you can at this very minute think of at least three instances today where you used sales and negotiation skills. This is a good thing. You'll need to hone those skills to negotiate great deals in real estate! Don't you wish they had taught you some of this in grade school?

Teaching kids sales and negotiation skills can change the world.

The U.S. job market is in trouble. We have spent decades sending our kids to school and we've been doing them wrong. Or rather, we have been teaching our children the wrong things by leaving important skills out of the curriculum. We send people out into the world to recognize only one opportunity: a J-O-B. We send them out to TAKE jobs, and we don't send them out with skills that would help them MAKE jobs. This is an imbalance. The job makers are fewer and fewer. Now what? I can promise you that people in our society will have to adapt or die. We will get to that line of thinking a little later in the book.

Education is important, but there is more than one type of learning. There is academic education, emotional education, financial education and spiritual education. We need to know how to apply our knowledge in all of these areas, no matter what we do in life, so we can have better communication with others and propel ourselves to a better lifestyle at every stage of life. We confuse these types of education with professional education, such as in becoming a doctor, lawyer, architect, an electrician or a financial planner. (Did you know that it takes longer to become an electrician than it does to become a financial planner? I'll get to that a bit later, too.) The point is

that professional education is just one piece of what we need, especially as real estate investors. As Michael Gerber – one of my mentors and one heck of an intelligent man – points out, with professional education you can become an excellent technician, but being a technician can stand in your way of achieving true success. Perhaps it is better to become a generalist.

Generalists have to understand sales and working with a team. For example, I am a generalist in real estate. I was pushed into this specialty by unfortunate events. However, I can look back and say that I am now grateful for those events. My wife is healthy and happy; my kids are all healthy and happy. Heck, I'm healthy and happy! How did we achieve this stature? We adapted… so we haven't died. I told you I would get to this.

Choose not to adapt and you will die.

If you are laid off from your job, you will have to adapt or the world will make a meal out of you. If you are suddenly put into a situation where you must take action to change your life and you don't take action, what will happen? You could actually cease to be. At the very least, your world as you know it will cease to exist. It's like walking around in Chicago year-round in summer clothes. Quite literally, you need to adapt to the changing weather and put on the right type of clothing or die. The same rule applies when one makes the shift from "employee" to "self-employed" to "entrepreneur." It is an adapt-or-die mentality. What will you do to survive? What will you do to feed your family? Will you take the action that is necessary to move forward?

As an employee, a lot of times all you have to be is "meat in the seat." I used to watch my fellow employees' behaviors closely. Many of them took smoke breaks. They took a lot of smoke breaks, which was irritating even after my short time on the job. I was a hard worker and I didn't smoke. I didn't take smoke breaks. I didn't take many breaks at all. The law says I could have 15 minutes in the morning before lunch and 15 minutes in the afternoon, but aside from lunch I didn't take many breaks. That was my choice, yes, but I didn't take smoke breaks, which is my point here. Yet I was paid the same as the smokers were. That arrangement didn't exactly motivate me to be the best employee I could be. It didn't seem to motivate the smokers either. They certainly weren't the best employees. Then again, why should they be ideal employees or strive harder when they'd be paid the same as harder workers? (And please don't send me nasty messages if you happen to be a smoker. You know that's not my point. Whether you smoke or not is entirely your choice. It is, in fact, your right.)

That lazy mindset is far from that which you must possess when you endeavor to go into real estate. First you have to accept the idea of self-employment. As Robert Kiyosaki points out in his Rich Dad Poor Dad books so well, in that quadrant you are responsible for managing your own time. Its likely you will put in more time every day "on the job" than when you were an employee. My employee training taught me how to use my time really well. For example, I was trained to be on

the phone for eight hours a day. People ask me how I could do that. I'm glad I had that experience. It taught me skills I call upon even today. Phone work is a part of what you do first as a self-employed person and certainly as a real estate investor. You will be talking to a lot of people!

The similarity between the W-2 employee and the self-employed individual is that they are both working for a check. The employee receives a paycheck regularly every two weeks. The self-employed person receives payment from clients and customers. It is anything but regular pay, but it is the same as a paycheck if you think about it. However, many self-employed people are also entrepreneurs and they possess a high level of entrepreneurial spirit. That is an excellent character trait!

As an investor you are an entrepreneur who doesn't receive a paycheck of any kind. As an entrepreneur, you are creating value that others can use. It might be money and it might be jobs or affordable housing. In centuries past, maybe you could have learned your investing and entrepreneurial skills as an apprentice, but not now. Before the advent of the corporation and the ideal of employees and "on-the-job" training, we learned in apprenticeships under a master. I wish that were still the case. But now people want to be paid to teach and even paid to learn (considering they learn on the job as they are receiving a regular paycheck). It should instead be about creating value to get value.

My jobs in sales taught me important lessons. I remember my very first day in sales. That's when I realized that if I didn't

sell I also didn't eat! However, I had to do my job in sales with integrity. I could not use tactics I saw others using, because I had to earn money in my sales job honestly. It's just who I am. In fact, I've lost jobs because I couldn't or wouldn't do my job using the tactics that my superiors wanted me to use. We are talking about retail sales where I was selling on the floor. We're talking about selling to complete strangers and selling them something they may not know they need. Up until I became a sales person, I thought I had to take a course and earn a certification to be a good sales person. That was an assumption.

Don't make assumptions.

I made an assumption that I couldn't be in sales because I didn't have the "right" training. People make assumptions all the time. I hear, "I can't do X, Y or Z, because I don't have a license!" I tell them they need to turn that around and make a question out of that statement. Ask, "HOW can I do 'it' without a license?" We set ourselves up for failure because of the way we talk to ourselves and by making assumptions. Stop it. Ask more questions. Be a person of integrity, too.

Integrity means more than just doing what you say you're going to do when you tell others you will do it. Integrity means not lying to yourself either. Let's take something simple. Let's talk about getting up in the morning. Say you told yourself that you would get up at 6:00 a.m. The next morning rolls around and you don't get up till 6:02 a.m. Yes,

28

it's just two minutes, but guess what? You said 6:00 and you didn't do what you said you would do. You didn't have integrity about doing what you told yourself you would do. How can others believe you if YOU don't believe you?

Integrity goes hand in hand with character. We will go more deeply into the importance of character soon enough, but for now just stick with me. Something you may not have noticed but I know you happen to appreciate is dealing with businesses and people who have good character and integrity. For example, do you have a friend who is annoyingly on time all the time? This person does what he/she says he/she is going to do. That's called character, which also happens to be one of the secret business-building ingredients. To do well in your real estate BUSINESS, you will develop character, which simply means that your "yes" means "yes" and your "no" means "no." Could you imagine if every company stood behind its products all the time, no matter what, and they develop the reputation for always saying yes, and the customer is always right? Do you know of a company like that? Do you like that company? Do you refer your friends and family to that company? Sure you do.

If you do that in your business, people will come back and will gladly pay for that extra customer service and peace of mind. That's something you can do. It's something you can implement inside of any business, especially real estate. Stand behind the services that you offer.

Think about it. If you promise to be able to close escrow on time, you then do everything in your power to close escrow on time. If you promise that you can open escrow on time, and you have the earnest money it takes to do it, then show up on time. These simple actions go a long way in helping you get deals that ordinarily you might not be able to obtain. Why? Real estate investing is a small world. You treat people right and they'll tell everyone they know about you. You treat people wrong and that will be their message to the world.

Once you're living in integrity, the next thing you need to do is learn to set clear boundaries. This is just one more example of emotional intelligence. By setting boundaries with other people, you can avoid drama, trauma and issues. I take what I do seriously. I don't have room in a deal for someone else's emotional reactions. One way to avoid this scenario in which you or another person will get upset is by establishing boundaries and being clear about the rules. You can do this assertively (not aggressively – and there is a huge difference). This goes for my team, too. If I'm paying someone to provide me with solutions, that's what I expect. Not drama and issues. If I've set my expectations and theirs correctly and clearly, there will be no drama.

Do you want an example of how we deal with each other in my team? This is best shown by what an associate jotted down one day while sitting with me at a park. Our time was interrupted by a call I had to take from my team, because we were closing another deal. I knew my team and I work together well, because we address drama head on. However, I didn't realize in words how this looked from the outside. I

asked my friend if I could share what she wrote. She agreed. This is directly from her notes:

"Watching J. negotiate a deal is a thing of beauty. He is relaxed and confident. It seems like nothing ruffles his feathers. He remains cool and collected, no matter the size of the deal and any hiccups that come with it. He is very clear with his directives and boundaries. He sets expectations with ease. By being clear and direct, J. makes all members of his team work harder and perform their best. If there are misunderstandings they can be discussed and fixed. From negotiating rents to discussing taxes and fees, everything can be worked out.

I watched J. in a discussion involving occupancy of an apartment complex and he spoke with great emotional intelligence that moved me to write my observations. Further he displays tremendous financial intelligence and has a business savvy that the best educated among us can't sometimes achieve. At the end of the call, everyone was happy with the content, terms and the relationships. There is no room for miscommunication when working in a team, and there is no room for drama. There is no room for a change in terms that have been agreed upon either. J. taught me these things simply from listening to him on a call. He says, 'Letting things go unaddressed is never the solution.' He's right.

J. also knows the power of publicly praising team members for a job well done and for their strengths. I witnessed this, too. He believes in rewarding people for performance. He takes input from all members of his team; he gets people to talk to

> *each other in an open and honest manner. When everyone is clear in a goal, the goal will be met. Greater communication provides for better negotiations. J. infuses humor into his conversations, too, which puts people at ease and puts J. on the winning side of negotiations. J. and each member of the team practice integrity. I found myself wanting to do business with J. immediately after witnessing this call, which was an unintended outcome!"*

I included my associate's words to make a point. She knows that I'm going to do what I say when I say it. My team will do the same. Who wouldn't want to deal with a real estate investor or anyone else for that matter who embraces and puts into practice these skills in every transaction? It is part of being an emotionally intelligent person that understands getting what we want means giving what others need. Emotional intelligence is absolutely critical in financial deals. People don't entrust big money with you because of your financial savvy. It's about trust and your ability to understand situations. They can see that you know how to handle dramas and traumas, and how to respond appropriately. They want to deal with you because you have shown that you won't lose your head, no matter what.

If I get wrapped up in the emotions around a deal, for example, when a building catches fire, it wouldn't work well for my investors and it sure won't work well for me. I have to be calm. As an investor you have to be calm. Period. The people entrusting me with their money need to know that I can calmly handle delays, contractor issues and more. I

can handle a fire. I know I can, because one of my buildings burned down... TWICE. (Yes, we'll get to that.)

If we lose our emotional intelligence (if we lose our calm) we turn a temporary problem into a permanent problem. Then we have to take responsibility for our actions. We will then have to relive the events and our actions over and over. That creates a whole new set of problems. It's a bad cycle that is best to be avoided. It's better to see a problem as temporary, be aware of what's going on and adjust your sails to create smoother sailing. Developing our emotional intelligence is a continual learning process. Everything changes. You need to learn to adapt and never jump to conclusions. Emotional intelligence dictates that you look at things calmly and rationally. That keeps you from jumping to conclusions or reacting too quickly. Give people the benefit of the doubt until you find out otherwise. There is usually an explanation for anything that goes wrong in a deal. It's better to use your efforts and energies in positive ways.

Being a person of integrity helps me to succeed in business. Without integrity, emails become a sales-prevention machine, and being a successful real estate investor requires good sales skills delivered with integrity. It is important to sell your message with integrity and sincerity. Further, to do well in sales you have to 1) generate your own leads and 2) cultivate relationships. Once you have built relationships and trust with your leads, it is up to you to then close the sale and get referrals. If it weren't for referrals, I would never have done as many deals as I have! Closing real estate deals takes something that other forms of investing don't. That's interpersonal skills (a.k.a., people skills).

Along with people skills that come to you through emotional intelligence, being an investor in real estate requires really good listening skills. Street smarts certainly don't hurt! I have a lot of street smarts, but the other skills I learned and developed over time. I had to commit myself to my dream and I knew that to get there would require new skills. For example, I wasn't always comfortable with speaking to other human beings, much less speaking to sizeable groups of individuals. Against my will, I decided (that's code for my mentor said I should do this, but I didn't want to) that I had to get over my anxieties about public speaking, so I joined Toastmasters. In no time, I had learned these new skills and got to practice public speaking every week. The group gave me excellent feedback and I adjusted to become a pretty good speaker. I'm still learning, but now I enjoy the speaking part. I can talk to anyone about real estate investing, business and life. I've learned to be an excellent listener, which as I said is a necessity. If you're always busy talking, talking, talking... how are you going to hear what the other person has to say? You'll miss a lot if you are more about hearing yourself talk than hearing the other person's responses to your questions. But then, I wasn't always the best listener and I had to learn how to approach potential investment partners.

I'll never forget one of my first lessons on listening.

While prospecting one day I cornered a guy and went into
what I THOUGHT was a good elevator pitch. The man
listened politely as I rambled on. At the end, he simply asked,
"Would you like to sell more? You have to learn to say less to
a greater number of people." Not too long after that I learned
about the 70/30 rule: Listen 70% of the time and ask great
questions the other 30%. Simply put, you have to listen more.
Today, this active listening skill is something I share in my
sales training classes. I can give you the meat of that class in
two words: JUST LISTEN. Then the other person's problem
can be solved, because you heard it.

Here's an example: Say you're talking to a woman who is a
homeowner and also in an abusive relationship. She wants
to leave, but she feels stuck. This conversation actually
happened to me. A woman told me that she was in an abusive
relationship and wanted out but felt stuck. All I really did was
listen to her. I wanted to help her and thought I might buy
the house. However, that wasn't a good solution because she
didn't want to remain "stuck" for 90 days through the closing
process. If she wanted to be free in short time, she needed a
faster exit plan. I knew that I could close in seven days. She
said that if she could A, B, C and D, she would be free. All she
needed was $X and she could go. All I did was listen so I could
provide a solution. I became a solution to her big problem.
She unfortunately decided to stay in the relationship and the
house, but I've used that solution in other situations to solve

problems (using not one dime of my own cash). That brings us to a question I hear consistently.

How do you raise private capital?

I wish I had $10 for every time I get asked this question. We will get into this skill a little later on. For now, I'll leave you to think about my approach. Once again, it has to do with interpersonal skills, active listening and emotional intelligence. When I approach someone about becoming a backer of a real estate deal, for example, a very large deal like those I do now that might require (in this example) an investment of $1M, I ask them one question that works every time: "When would you like me to stop sending you the $100K check?" Why $100K? That is 10% of the $1M investment. You can do the math. If the investor gives me $1M and I give him the $100K every year in passive income, how long would it take for him to get his investment back and how much could he make beyond that amount over time? There is no magic. It's math. Like a good friend always says to me, "Do the math and the math will tell you what to do." He is so right!

How did I get to this point where I'm so comfortable in asking for large sums? Over time! Again, no magic. Sorry. Just hard work, lots of learning experiences and a whole bunch of mistakes have given me the confidence to do the deal and then do more. I will share with you, however, that I didn't always have the confidence I do now. Would you believe me if I were to tell you that my journey started with a Vision Book? (Okay,

and a weeklong crash course in real estate investing. That was pretty important.)

My "magic" vision and me...

As you now know, things weren't great in my life at the time I became a real estate investor. Through a series of not-so-wonderful events, my family and I were displaced and starting over. That was in 2008. I knew something had to change. ME! I had to change how I looked at things. I made a conscious choice of becoming a real estate investor. I was sponsored into a short course in real estate... There was just enough money to pay for ONE week. I learned quickly that I had to Move at the Speed of Instruction™ and to ask a whole lot of questions. I didn't know this made me a little different than the other people in the room, but it did. I want you to be different, too, so listen up here. This next bit is crucial.

Again, I had just one week to learn everything I could about real estate investing and the different types of deals to be had. We covered a lot of ground in a short time. I had to implement anything I learned right away. As I sat in that weeklong course, if the presenter gave the class a concept of how to do something, I'd do it right away... while on a 15-minute break! I'd take my phone to the hallway, make a call and put into action what I had just learned. This had an amazing result. If it worked, I could immediately report my results. If it didn't, I could ask questions and adjust my approach.

You may already understand that information (i.e., knowledge) is only the first step. To get good at something you have to apply that knowledge. That's what I was doing in real time! I learned that if I am in a learning environment and I learn cool things but I wait till I get home to start implementing my new knowledge, it's not going to work well. What do you think could happen? I could forget things or how a process worked, I might let anxiety about "not doing it right" get to me and stop me, or I just might not take action at all. Isn't that the way it works at some seminars? You get so loaded down with information and concepts that you can freeze up. I couldn't allow that to happen. My family counted on me to get it right, implement and succeed. We had to eat. I had to make this work. Please remember this phrase: "Done is better than perfect."

That week I became a real estate investor and I haven't stopped. I took a lot of action steps. I left clever cards on cars night after night after night, inviting those who might have properties to sell or who might want to buy real estate or learn about real estate investing to contact me. Over time, my base of leads developed to a point that it was hard to keep up. I attended networking meetings, and I got my elevator pitch down to a few brief sentences:

"Hi, my name is J. Massey and I am a wholesaler. What that means is, I buy property at a discount and I sell property at a discount. What type of investing are you looking to do?" (This is my exact pitch.)

38

Next, I chose my "office" location. It's the same office I use to this day. Starbucks! I have my iPad, my iPhone and my "iBrain." Just joking. I take my brain everywhere. Oh, and my camera. I always have my camera! The rest is history. I make deals of all sizes, larger and larger all the time, every week because I am now recognized as a great problem solver in real estate. This is especially true in Memphis, but I will get to that story soon enough.

What's this about a Vision Book?

There is one tool that I used to help me make the necessary shift in my mindset that would ALLOW me to see that I could achieve what I wanted. I could get to my goals because I made sure to put these goals down on paper in a way that I could see them any time I felt like it. This is something I continue to do to this day and it still helps me. My dreams and goals may have grown, but I still need to SEE them. What's great is that this tool is something you can easily create for yourself. It has an amazing purpose. What am I talking about? It's my Vision Book! My Dream Book, if you will.

Have you ever heard that if you see it in your mind, you can receive it in your life? Believe it. I am living proof. Call it Law of Attraction. I don't care what you call it. Take this action step now... today. Grab a simple notebook and get to work! Make what you want in your life real to you. Create a list of things you want in your life. While there may be a lot of creature comforts, a more comfortable life and doodads that you don't actually need, be sure to add really big goals, like starting 12 charities. Notice I didn't say just one charity. I'm telling you to THINK BIG and have BIG DREAMS!

Next, collect up pictures of these things and write notes in your book. For me it was not a huge item that made it into the first pages of my Vision Book. It was a microwave oven. That's right. I wanted a decent microwave oven and a flash

drive on a keychain. That may sound strange to you, because today flash drives are everywhere and they are inexpensive. In 2008, they were relatively new to me. I found pictures of what I desired and I glued them into my Vision Book. I looked at them often. I'm happy to say that I did indeed get these doodads and I reached a lot of my early goals. I'm working on new goals now.

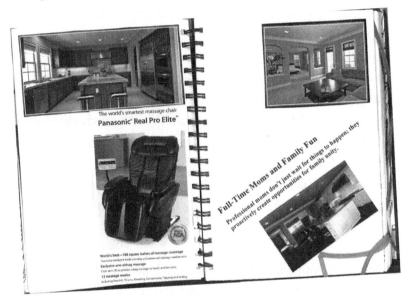

When you think about the things you want in your life, even small things, first list them out and then find pictures that you can cut out and put into your Vision Book. It's not the items themselves that you should focus on, but rather what they represent. These items represent certain things. For example, I added the amount of $625K in my book, because that's the amount I wanted to gather to invest in property… and I didn't know it at the time, but I was shooting low with that number. I love a good kitchen, so I added a picture of a really nice kitchen with modern, clean lines. I wanted nicer clothes, because I wanted all my clothes to be dry-cleaned. I also wanted a yellow Lamborghini. When I eventually test-drove that vehicle, I realized it wasn't a good fit for me... literally. As a very tall man, I didn't fit into my dream car. I adjusted my dream to what I drive now, which is an equally nice vehicle, but not nearly as flashy. It's an Audi S8 and I love driving it. What was the point of putting things in my Vision Book? To remind me why I was working so hard and to keep me motivated toward my goals. If I ever questioned myself or had a weak moment or felt defeated, I'd open my book and I was good to go again. It moved me back to the mindset I needed so I could keep taking action. When you create your Vision Book, I'd love for you to send me snapshots of some of the pages. Share them on my Facebook page at http://www. facebook.com/cashflowdiary. (Keep it clean, people. This is a real exercise.) Or email them to me from the website at http:// www.cashflowdiary.com.

By the way, your Vision Book can be a lead generator if you use it right. Keep it out on the table and see what happens. If people strike up a conversation with you about it, guess what? You might be creating leads right then and there. Be sure to get any real estate-minded person's information. Most people have a card. Don't just give them yours. It's best to get their information... and then follow up with them. Ask them about their dreams.

Allow yourself to dream!

Do me a favor... Do yourself a favor. NEVER stop dreaming! If you don't want to create a Vision Book, maybe a Vision Board (or even bulletin board) is more your style. I chose a book because I want to keep my book with me so I can look through it or add to it at a moment's notice. The book is practical. Most of us are mobile and on the run. We need something we can carry easily. You can't carry a board around with you. You could, but it's going to look strange and be cumbersome. You want to be able to use something on the fly, so a book is perfect. You can even jot down notes in it and talk about what you learned from mistakes. The Cashflow Foundation I am building has helped me to keep dreaming. Reading Robert Kiyosaki's books helped me tremendously. The Vision Book keeps my thoughts in the right place. All of these things serve as motivators.

No matter how you slice it, you have to see your goals and what you want in your life before you can take action steps to achieve these things. A simple way to help yourself is with the Vision Book:

Step 1: Make a list of things you want

Step 2: Put that list in order of importance

Step 3: Gather pictures, cut them out and put them in your book

Step 4: Carry your Vision Book with you everywhere you go and refer to it often

Step 5: Keep adding to the book and keep expanding your goals

Think about it. What would it take to own a home that has a price tag with a lot of commas? You would do X, Y and Z. Figure out the steps. Take action. Continue to dream. Make your dreams bigger. Raise your standards from small to large dreams. In my case, I went from dreaming about single-family homes to multi-unit complexes to retail malls to commercial properties to high rises, then toll roads, parking garages and fairgrounds. Now I even think about investing in jails! Do I have all these things yet? No. But I'm taking the necessary action steps, because I know what it all comes down to is INSPIRED ACTION!

You might already know what you want out of life. You might even have a Vision Book and you have already clipped pictures and pasted them into place. You might even be able to get yourself to the mindset that all things are possible. (They are, you know!) But then you feel a dip in your inspiration. How do you get it back, or maybe how do you get it to begin with? I hear this question sometimes. The only thing I can tell you is to never let the dip stop you from taking action or to overwhelm you. Push yourself even when you don't feel like doing something. Never let the HOW stop you. Look around you. What do you see? A garden? Nope. I see real estate. A movie theatre? Nope. Real estate. The high-rise apartment building across the street? Nope. Real estate!

Understand this, too. You will never be perfect, there is no such thing as a perfect deal in real estate and things WILL go wrong. That's okay. Mistakes are simply feedback for doing

44

things better the next time. Be willing to fail forward, fail often and just go through the experience. I promise that you'll live.

I want you to be inspired, but to keep that inspiration and then take action steps. Don't just go out and buy the things you want even if you have the cash to do so. You must THINK DIFFERENTLY. I want you to believe that if you want X you can have X. To get there, you need to offer a product or service that solves problems. The bigger the problem the bigger the solution and the more money you have the potential to earn. Bigger problems equal more value in your solution. Think about transportation and telecommunication. At one time these were massive problems. Those who provided solutions were rewarded financially and they could have in their lives what they wanted.

The Vision Book is to keep you inspired and start the transformation process in your thinking and your life. The book you are reading now is a part of my ongoing transformation as I continue to be a better problem solver. Thinking and learning become the transforming mechanisms. As your beliefs change and your viewpoints broaden you will realize how much you are capable of doing. Just be careful in how you work forward in your Vision Book. This is not a wish list that you can buy your way through. Let me explain.

I remember speaking to a woman once who told me she really wanted a puppy. It was a special breed of puppy and it wasn't cheap. She added it to her Vision Book. Later I ran into the woman again and she was thrilled to tell me that she

BOUGHT the puppy. NO! That's not what the Vision Book is all about. I'm glad she was so inspired to add the puppy to her list, but the idea wasn't to spend her money to buy a dog. She missed the point, but at least she was enthusiastic. She didn't get the puppy by taking any action steps. The woman hadn't changed the way she looked at things. Her mindset hadn't budged. She didn't go through any experiences other than going to the pet shop and making a purchase. She helped no one solve a problem through real estate and she didn't practice any of my teachings. (Sigh…)

Let me inspire YOU!

My vision is bigger that just my time on the planet and how it affects my family and me. Working from a place of true inspiration, I intend to help you and a whole bunch of people like you. I plan to help people who aren't anything like you, too! This is what the book is about. I want to inspire you to the greatness that you may or may not see in yourself. Then I hope that you will pay it forward to inspire others. Take action. That's it. If you want to inspire, you have to take action and be inspiring. People love to be around action-takers! Go after your goals with tenacity. There are no short cuts. This book isn't going to give you short cuts to wealth. I guarantee you that to achieve your goals in real estate, one of which is probably a much healthier bank account with a lot more commas and zeros; you will have failures… or rather "failure events." I can also tell you that you will likely achieve results different from those you intended. You will learn to ask

better questions than you know to do in the beginning. The questions are actually the answers you seek!

Questions really are the answers.

I ask a lot of questions and, as a result, people tell me all about their problems that I can solve. You can say that I actively look for problems now, so I can provide the solutions. If entertainment is a problem, why not put a movie theater in the space in question? Or a bookstore, PC gaming center or even a gym? Hey, that's entertainment to some. Look at the area and figure out the type of entertainment people might want. Solve that problem.

I can hear you right now. Yes, J., but I'm not you. I don't even know how to look at problems like that. How do I get to your level of thinking? Practice! That's how. Get yourself out there and practice your interpersonal skills. Practice listening. Get comfortable in talking to people. Get comfortable in asking questions and then just be quiet and let the prospects talk. GET RID OF THE AGENDA PLAYING IN YOUR HEAD. If you are just waiting for your turn to speak so you can dazzle others with your silver tongue, you serve no one. You solve no problems. You aren't listening. If you need to develop these skills, I have a fantastic idea. Play Robert Kiyosaki's Cashflow 101 board game! Yes, a game.

Playing Cash Flow 101 built my business.

One thing that helped me understand different strategies in
real estate investing is playing Robert Kiyosaki's Cashflow
101 game. Through playing with different groups of people
I learned how deals can be done in a lot of different ways,
not just in the game but in real life. It takes discipline to
ignore other players and to realize you aren't playing against
them but rather teaching yourself to win in real-world real
estate. The game taught me about cash flow in a big way. The
equation of $200/mo. in passive income multiplied by 12
months equaling $2,400 started embedding itself in my brain.
Every asset (real estate) can bring passive income. Every type
of deal brings its own rewards and issues. After I played the
game a few times, I was sold more than ever before on the fact
that I would be not just a real estate investor but a really, really
successful investor! So far, so good.

"Wealth is a team sport!" I heard that from entrepreneur Jim
Bunch. He's right. Everything is a team sport if you think
about it, because no one really accomplishes anything alone.
Just like in tennis, there is a player and a coach. There are
others who help the player perform at his/her best. There are
even the youngsters who are in charge of dashing across the
court to pick up the loose balls. If you can't quite grasp the
importance of this concept, play the Cashflow game. It has a
way of forcing you to understand that you can do more with
a team mindset than with a self-centered way of thinking. The
game also teaches you about the different types of intelligence.
Remember how I mentioned those types earlier in the book?

I could test you here… ask you which types of intelligence I listed. Okay, I'll give it to you: Academic, Emotional, Financial and Spiritual. It is a well-rounded person who possesses all of these. Most people are lacking in one or more areas, however.

For example, some people have emotional intelligence, but they lack financial intelligence. Maybe they have emotional intelligence and book smarts (academic intelligence). They may do well in certain areas of their life, but one needs financial intelligence when it comes to making good decisions in real estate investing. However, if you have financial intelligence and other people possess other forms of intelligence, maybe you can work together as a team to get deals done. Again, the Cashflow game proves this theory.

If you aren't familiar with Robert Kiyosaki's Cashflow game, let me break it down for you. It's a board game that requires active participation, and you have to pay attention to what's going on at all times. On the inside of the board there is a circle that represents the rat race we're all in until we change our mindset to allow ourselves to participate in real estate investing. Through a series of good decisions and working in a team with other players, you can get out of the rat race and onto the "fast track" that is the outer path on the board. The plastic game pieces come in different colors of rats and chunks of cheese. You place your cheese on your dream goal that you choose from the outer fast track. Some seem more popular than others. Ultimately I see players place their cheese on the Mediterranean Sea Cruise. Hey, it's a great goal on the board and in life. Why not?

The point is that the decisions we make in the game reflect what we do in real life. At least the same rules apply. Our choices get us where we are in life. Our choices will change our path. Our decisions and how we use the knowledge we have gained along the way get us to our goals. In the Cashflow game you learn how to use a profit-and-loss (P&L) statement, which at first might be overwhelming. Once you understand it, however, it's not such a big deal. You can handle it. You are stronger and smarter than a piece of paper.

If you learn how to use the P&L statement in the game, you can translate that information to real life. You start looking at things a little differently. You start weighing out your earnings and expenses. You understand why doodads are not necessary. Though they might be in your Vision Book it doesn't mean you have to spend money to buy them. These doodads might not be nearly as important as you think. The P&L statement helps you understand the real profits you are earning from your real estate investments in the game, and that also translates to life. Thus, learning to make sound investments plays into the bigger picture when you get out there in the real world to make deals. But how do you decide what is a good

and what is a bad investment? We get to that later in the book. For now, let's talk more about the game and how learning it benefits your understanding of the real-world investment community.

In the game you learn to take risks. You learn to work WITH other players. This is different from what I learned growing up. "Play to win." That's what my mom always said when we played board games growing up in my family. If I said I played to win things were cool. Now I play to win in real life, but I get there by working with other people. It's that way in the Cashflow game. In no other way are you going to learn how to make deals. You must work with the other players.

It's funny to watch people play the game. One of the first things that happens is that they are assigned a profession. In the game, the first time you'll see an emotional reaction is when people randomly and blindly choose their profession card. You'll hear, "Yes! I'm a doctor!" On the opposite end of the spectrum the person who picks the janitor card isn't so excited. You ultimately hear crickets or a groan. The game simulates the good and bad of life. That includes professional choices. The game forces us to make decisions. Sometimes I institute a clock wherein players have only 30 seconds to make a decision. I watch people's faces. They panic, but then they make decisions quickly. I do this because we make decisions every day of our lives. We need to learn to make them quickly and stop over-thinking.

In the game other types of investments come up besides real estate. There are a lot of emotion-evoking things that come up, too, aside from the profession cards. There are stocks that you can buy. That is an emotional decision. You can go bankrupt, you can have babies and you can end up having to buy all sorts of doodads, or rather you are forced to buy them by picking that card. When these things come up the responses are always emotional in the players. Their reactions in the game show me how they will likely react to stimuli and challenges in their lives.

Life can be challenging. If you want something, you may have to overcome obstacles to get it. Obstacles will inevitably get in your way. If you tell me you give up in the Cashflow game then I know that's how you act in real life. That's why your life isn't working for you as well as you wish it would. While you're playing the game, your fears are on display. Even though it's a simulated play environment, you tend to use the same emotions that you do in real life when working deals. We need to take a risk sometimes, especially in real estate. But you say, "What if I fail?" Even in the game, you say it. If this is your mindset, I'm here to tell you that you are letting this fear rob you of experiencing emotional intelligence. Think about it this way... Donald Trump rose in the public eye and failed in the public eye, and then he rose again. Without emotional intelligence all the other types of intelligence mean nothing.

What else does the Cashflow game give you?

The Cash Flow game leads to networking, which in turn leads to referrals. There is no better lead generator! If you want to be in the real estate arena, play this game. Host games at your home or in your clubhouse. You will leave smarter than when you arrived. You play the game to gain financial intelligence. Then, once you know the game well, you can teach it. After all, he who educates the market dominates the market! There is a great truth in this saying.

I have been teaching the game for a decade now. I connect people to the fact that they can become what I have become as a real estate investor. My success is a natural extension of the game. People ask how do I do "it," or can I do "it" with you and can I learn from you? Sometimes the people I play the game with end up investing in my real estate deals. Or we work together on deals. It's exciting! I can honestly say that the Cashflow game helped me build my business. My largest game so far involved leading 180 people in how to play. I've done it internationally on a boat twice, once with Robert Kiyosaki! At the time of this writing, I was just asked to lead the game for a third time on the cruise. It's called Summit at Sea™, an annual investor's cruise. It's fun, I get to meet a lot of interesting, intelligent people who accomplish a lot in their lives and I get to run workshops, participate in educational round tables and lead a big board game that I enjoy. With this in mind, it makes me smile when people ask me what it is about real estate that gets me so passionate. If I hadn't become a real estate investor, I wouldn't have had so many exciting and wonderful experiences. Hey, I can tell you… I am

GRATEFUL! You know who else is grateful? My wife, Popi. I want to share her viewpoint about playing Cashflow 101 and how it changed her mindset. This is important because she and I are a team.

In Popi's Words...

Cash flow and passive income are important because it means that we have money coming in without having to work over and over and over again for it. It means that we can take time off with our family without having to worry about whether or not income is coming in, and it means that we have made our money work for us as opposed to us working for our money.

Entrepreneurship is important to our family because in the Bible it talks about entrepreneurs as being those who would serve before kings. It talks about entrepreneurs, for example, as you will find in Proverbs 31, which is about a woman entrepreneur. She had her own business. This is interesting to me, because today some are lead to believe that the Bible demeans women. It's really the opposite as proven by this proverb in which women who are entrepreneurs and business owners are lifted up. Today, a lot of women have to generate income on their own without having to rely on a husband or a man. So Proverbs 31 actually speaks to us today about entrepreneurship. Men and women!

In our home we practice entrepreneurship not just for ourselves but also for our kids. We have three girls and a boy. We want all of them to know they can make something of themselves in the world via entrepreneurial thinking. However, we didn't

always think in these terms. It's only when I started playing the Cashflow 101 game that I began to understand. This game freed my mind. I was in the path of go to school, get a good education and get a good job. What I learned in my 12 years as a recruiter was that in the end just because you have a good education doesn't necessarily mean that you have the skills to perform the job you want. A good education doesn't teach social skills either. Social skills are very, very important as far as where you're going to work. And not only as an entrepreneur. If you choose to have a W-4 position, let's face it… people enjoy working with people they like, people who are able to get along with others, people with good social skills.

The Cashflow 101 game is important because, again, it freed me from thinking that getting a W-4 job is the only way to generate an income. Playing the game helped me understand that I was timid in regard to taking risks. It taught me that I didn't really know what to do with the money I had. It taught me different ways to help my money work for me, which is so much better than my working for my money! I squirreled my money away in a bank. Back in the '80s and '90s, when interest rates were at 13%, maybe that was a great idea, but now you get maybe 2% if you're lucky. How does putting money in the bank like that make sense today?

Like the Bible says, instead of burying our money in the ground and being fearful, we should put it to use and let it grow so we can do more for others. Cashflow 101 taught me how to fulfill the Bible scripture that talks about how if God gives you five talents, you go out and make five more, and if he gives you ten, you go out and make ten more. I never really understood what that meant until I started playing this board game. The scripture is telling me that by creating the talents, I can provide a way for me (for myself and for my kids) to take risks with money without a lot of consequences. Sure, this is emotional and you get plenty emotional playing this game, but that's not a life-threatening consequence. Risk is a part of success. I don't know any successful people who didn't take risk. God knows, J. and I took risks and we have certainly reaped rewards as entrepreneurs. I know I can care for my family and myself as an entrepreneur. This is truly empowering, and the board game helped me to deal with my fear… to not let fear stop me from taking a few risks.

God gave me talents that I can use to take care of my family. The board game allowed me to do that without fear. It propelled me in the right direction. Even as a busy mother of three toddlers, I started my own business with Pampered Chef. It's a Plan B in my mind, and I absolutely love the company! Why a Plan B? Because of all the personal and financial issues J. and I faced in our lives, I learned that a Plan B is very important. I will never worry about where the money will come from again, because I'm part of that solution. I want to make a note here about Robert and Kim Kiyosaki. It was through my conversations with them that I pushed my fears and excuses aside (and I can tell you I had plenty of excuses, from being a busy mom to just not feeling ready) to start my business. They are very direct people who taught me that there is no reason to pussyfoot around issues. Just speak your mind assertively and take action steps. They did it; J. did it; and I

> *did it. Like J. says, there is no magic wand that will get you to your goals. It takes hard work, clearly defined goals and determination. Believe and you shall receive. The Bible isn't joking about that!*

Alright, I think you get the point. Just get started. Learn about real estate investing. Choose an area in which to begin – like wholesaling that I'll tell you about a bit later in the book. WRITE A DEAL THIS WEEK. (That's my personal challenge to you once you've finished reading this book and listened to my podcasts.) And play the Cashflow game!

Okay, right about now, you're getting impatient. You're asking, "J., so when do you get to the part about using none of your own money or credit to buy properties?" That's next. It's called CREATIVE ACQUISITIONS.

STEP TWO:

No money? No problem.

Your fears; your problem!

*"All riches have their origin in mind. Wealth is in ideas…
not money." Robert Collier.*

You've heard about people who buy real estate with no money
down or with none of their own money or credit. It's called
creative acquisitions and it happens every day in all sorts of
industries. It really does. Maybe up till now you've thought
that buying property with no money down isn't possible, but
you'd be wrong in that assumption. (Be careful about making
assumptions!)

You absolutely can purchase real estate using zero of your
own money or credit. How? Leveraging other people's money.
(You've heard of OPM, right?) And now you're shaking
your head. I'm here to tell you that I do this all the time. Up
to the date of this writing I have spent maybe $20K of my

own money in deals. The rest I have leveraged in a variety of ways though creative approaches. And it's not just money I leverage. It's other people's talents and skills, too. How do I get other people on board with my goals and vision? How can you? It boils down to your abilities as a good communicator, asker of good questions and good negotiator. Listening skills are a must!

Finding the funding you need for a real estate deal or really any business deal is not about technique. It's about recognizing the problems to be solved. Once you've gotten to the problem and you communicate a solution, people will ask you to "show me how you plan to make it happen."

You must recognize the problem. They [property buyer/seller and investor] have a problem. Not you. When you're new as a real estate investor, you have to be willing to subject yourself to the investor's needs. Substitute "needs" for "problems." Problems come in the form of: 1) taxes 2) protecting the capital, 3) growing the capital and more. In the latter, they want to make sure the money doesn't run out. This is of critical importance to the elderly who are looking at piles of cash vs. streams of income to leave to their heirs (who usually don't want to manage properties – they prefer the cash). How do you help people get to their investment goals and your goals at the same time?

There is a management component to making funds work for you. First, you must understand money! It is a TOOL for you to use to achieve an objective. It's just that. We can't freak out.

We can make it easier in our heads. For example, think about borrowing a pen from someone, even someone you don't know. You ask, "May I borrow a pen?" That's easy, right? Now say, "May I borrow money?" It's just a tool. You must use it to achieve a goal. (I'll get more into the asking part very soon.)

What you really need to understand about money is that it's just something to which we have assigned value. You need to understand how we assign value to things, including money and property. Even "bitcoins" have value because a group of people started trading these non-tangible things and assigned value to them. If you think about it, how is that so different from agreeing that the paper we use as currency is worth a certain value? Some people "mine" for bitcoins. They use their computers to actually generate bits of value that translate to actual dollar value in the real world. It's wild! But what's a bitcoin? Glad you asked. I have a video for that topic! I invite you to check out all the videos on my site at www.CashFlowDiary.com. You never know what type of information you'll walk away with. But let me be a spoiler here. The reason bitcoins became a topic of a video is because I saw in the news that a guy in Canada was trying to sell his house for bitcoins. I started thinking, hey, interesting idea. Why not? It could be done, and then I thought… I wonder how we could assign value in such a case? A bitcoin is a form of digital currency used to "buy" or trade goods and services online and even in the real world. It could work. I am watching this trend as markets spring up around bitcoins. You should, too. As a real estate investor, you need to keep an eye to trends like this.

You are NOT raising "money."

Raising private capital is not about raising "money." It is more than just gaining access to money. It's also about gaining access to people's skills, emotions and relationships. (This is what investing really is about – and then getting to the private capital.) And since we're talking about this, let me share with you that I'd rather have 15 broke people help me make something happen to execute my vision than a couple of the wrong investors who have a lot of money. It's who these 15 people know that will get me to the money.

We hear all the time "it takes money to make money." Well, it does, but it is what you call money that is the real issue. Intellectual capital IS the money. That's the idea that makes things happen. Representation of the fee is the realization of the value you created with your mind. Intellectual capital equates to value. Ideas are what we disassociate with these days, and that's incorrect thinking.

Think about this… We can't MAKE money. Only our government can do that. We as individuals can't. (It's illegal!) We can, however, EARN money by presenting ideas and enrolling people into our vision. That's how you raise private capital. Specifically, you can find private capital in:

• **Investors' 401K and retirement plans, mutual funds and savings.** Investing the money can bring excellent tax advantages and there are other advantages that can be considered.

62

• **Networking events.** When your message is delivered very clearly to investors in a room you have a good chance of creating leads.

• **Family and friends.** Also called "pillow investing" you can gather funds from people via their credit cards, retirement savings and plans, and bank savings accounts.

Understand that there is no "traditional" plan for finding private capital for real estate deals. It's what works best for the investor! One such plan that is good for elderly investors is a LEGACY PLAN in which money has to be left to heirs, but how is that going to happen? How can you help the investor? Does he have a lot of property that needs to be liquidated or turned into cash for heirs? Is there someone in his family who might be able to manage the properties? Likely that is going to be overwhelming, but this has to be discussed. Maybe an elderly person who has an apartment building needs help in MANAGING the problem. He would be willing to carry the note. You solved a problem. You now have property to sell. You didn't need to find funding.

People also have to stop trying to relay "the RETURN on the investor's money." Why? Because it's not just a return on the money. That can take awhile. It's a problem being solved. It's a better way to approach.

It's the Law of Management. You have to think in terms of money [cash flow] like this:

Most of our money goes toward the past and present vs. where it should go!

Investors have needs for their money YESTERDAY, TODAY, TOMORROW and NEVER. Understanding where they're at regarding their cash flow situation with this formula helps you solve their problems and get to the funding. For example, what is the investor's age? How does the deal fit their lifestyle, life and needs? You can offer a delay in payments [paying back] with the investment, which actually will help their situation and yours.

It's NOT about the return.

You have to understand higher-level concepts around money. I don't expect that you are going to learn the whole tax code, but you should understand the basic principles of tax-deferment or how taxes work on the side of the investor. You need to understand how getting long-term capital means tax savings over time. And then you need to be able to explain in terms your investors can understand, which means meeting

each of them where they are in their head. Letting go of control is an important concept to get the investor to also let go.

I have a mental checklist of questions I go through with every investor. I won't ask all of the questions if I know some don't fit. The questions have to be geared to that individual. For example, I might ask, "On the news, they're saying things are horrible. So why would you want to get into real estate investing now?" Their answer to this question gives me an idea of their mindset and what they really hope to accomplish. It tells me if they are a risk-taker or cautious. The answers are always interesting.

For those who tell me they are serious investors or want to get more into investing, I might ask, "Can you tell me the last five transactions you've done?" If the answer is NONE, I can follow up with, "What's held you back? You've known about real estate for years, so why now?" Their answers help me understand their motivation and allow me to help them better. I also have a series of qualifying questions to help me understand their mindset around money… specifically their money and how they feel about letting it go to me to use in a deal. By questions, I mean a conversation. We are just having a conversation.

In that conversation, I need to find out something important, which is who else is involved in the investor's decision-making? There is always someone else involved… even if it's the guy's cat! What I need to know is who helps them with money decisions and what will the investor decide if that other person says no? Will the investor go ahead anyway if he/she sees the deal as a great opportunity? I can then help the individual "rehearse" responses that will help the co-decision-maker come to the same conclusion.

The long and short of it is that if the investor I'm chatting with is going to move forward with me, his/her part will not just stop at giving me money to put into a deal so they can get returns on their investment over time. The other thing they will do is to bring me referrals. This happens all the time, and I'm grateful. Referrals are my bread and butter. When you're a real estate investor and you become known for solving problems, you'll get referrals, too. However, before you can get to the referrals, you're going to have to understand the different ways investors can find money for you and how to use it. For example, do you understand how 401K plans work?

Before someone forks over his/her 401K savings to you, should have a good understanding of the tax implications involved and how that can benefit the investor over time. When investment firms collect the 401K monies they are looking for financial returns. Broker fees that are often not tied to performance though some are (active money managed account), in many cases, are taken first. By allowing you to use their 401K money in an investment deal, investors can get the returns they want without paying the broker fees. And let me be clear… I'm not against compensating a person for work performed. All I am saying is that by being closer to the investment you have a greater chance of having more of your original principal in the deal and more of the earnings make it

back into Hip National Bank (that's your bank account).
In the traditional 401K-broker model, the investors (who have
IRAs and retirement plans) are allowing the firm to advertise
on the radio and TV with their money, which means the
investors are solving the firm's problems and not the other
way around. To me, it's a better idea to use that money for
a solid real estate investment and gain the benefits without
paying the broker fees. I've included a real-life story in the
back of the book in the "Q & A with J." section that will give
you a better idea of how this really works.

You don't have to be "fearless."

Before we get further into raising capital and what to do
with it, I need to go back to a point I made in the last step…
Overcoming your fears so that you can accept the fact that
you CAN be a real estate investor and a darned good one at
that. I'm going to drive that point home, because in moving
forward as a real estate investor it is absolutely necessary
to stop REACTING out of fear. People tell me that I am a
"fearless" investor. That makes me smile. Like I said before, I
experience fear just like the next guy. Fear doesn't go away just
because your bank account has a higher balance and you have
done a lot of real estate transactions. My response to fear has
changed, and yours will likely need some adjusting, too.

Let fear be a driver for you toward your success. Don't let
it stop you from being successful. Don't let it stop you from
trying. Don't let fear stop you from learning. And don't let it

67

stop you from negotiating deals in which you use none of your own money or credit. You might be surprised by how much of the deal a seller will carry or how many investment dollars you can gather from investors once you've been successful in sharing your vision with them! I hope at this point you are beginning to see that I am really not much different from you. Maybe the only difference is that I am doing what you want to do. If you don't have to bring any of your own money or credit to the table to do deals, what's stopping you from moving forward?

Let me remind you that when I became a real estate investor I had no money to invest and no property. I was squatting in what was once my property… my family's residence. Officially, we became squatters on February 13, 2008. What a great Valentine's Day gift, huh? I began my real estate investment training in a live seminar classroom setting on February 25, 2008. I had a week of very intensive training and then I was on my way. Though I received a lot of support from those who went through training with me and from the leaders of that training program, I still had a lot to learn. For example, I had to learn how to do the basic contracts and fill them out correctly. Why? Like I said, I had to find a way to feed my family. I had run out of options, so I had to make real estate work for me. After all, I didn't have a college degree and I couldn't go back to the financial planning world because I didn't have $2M of assets under management in my book of business, which is a prerequisite for the position. I don't know if I chose real estate or if it chose me, but it has given me freedom I could never have achieved working for someone

else. I can be with my wife and kids. I can travel and I can spend time practicing my photography, which is one of my passions (as anyone who knows me can tell you).

I entered the world of real estate investing in February and I closed my first deal four months later on June 18, 2008. That's not to say it was the first offer on a property that I had written. Quite the contrary. I wrote several offers before I closed this deal in California. I still own this property, too. I get a rent check every month like clockwork. Three weeks after that deal came 11 more in a matter of one week. I had become good at what I was doing, which was primarily wholesaling.

Wholesaling is a great way to start.

Wholesaling is the most important strategy to learn, practice or at least understand in real estate investing, but before I got into this area of investing I tried other things. I tried short sales, but doing them and making them work requires a lot of detailed work and management. (Why are they called "short" sales when they take so darned long?) That's not really me. It doesn't suit who I am as an investor. It is not my "investor identity." I had to rely on my strengths, so I asked myself a question. "What am I good at doing?"

I was good at finding discounted properties and selling them at a discount to someone else while still making a profit. I had no clue about how to turn this into a lucrative venture, but I knew that I had to learn new skills. If I could learn how to do this effectively, then my life and the lives of my family members would be better. It's a lot like learning to tie our shoes. No one pays us to tie our shoes, but if I were to tell you that I'd give you $50 for every pair of shoes you tie, I'll bet that you'd be the best darned shoe-tier around. If then you realized that you could pay a friend $20 to tie shoes and you got to keep $30 without doing anything, I'm betting you'd be calling a lot of friends and having them tie shoes. The same rule applies in wholesaling real estate or finding other people who are willing to invest with you. You are using their money to fund the down payments and improvements (rehabbing) on your deals. Welcome to the world of real estate, a proven concept because everyone needs a place to live, work, play and lay! I'll get into this in a minute, too. First, let me tell you more about how I came to be a top wholesaler.

I started weeding out the different types of real estate investing to find my passion. I actually entered real estate investing via tax deed sales and I learned that I didn't like the auction process. I was ready for quick transactions. Tax deeds are not quick. I tried my hand at fixing and flipping. That didn't work out well. I then moved into doing short sales. I could easily deal with the emotional events that take place in short sales. During my time as an employee in financial planning I was accustomed to listening to people share their emotions with me. Dealing with the emotions in short sales wasn't the hard part. There was a lot of paperwork in short sales, and I didn't like that aspect. Being involved in short sales felt like a job. That's when I found wholesaling. I love wholesaling! I am under a certain time pressure with wholesaling, and I have to make the deal work. I realized

that I didn't need partners to get the job done, but I did see the need to gather a good team, because I was doing so many deals so quickly it got harder and harder to keep up. I needed help. Notice I said "team" and not partners.

I tried the partnership thing when I did my first fix 'n' flip. I found out I was more the fix 'n' flopper! I talk about this more in a later section of the book, but this fix 'n' flop deal was one of my big mistakes. Obviously I recovered and it was a heck of a good learning experience. It cost me hundreds of thousands of dollars because I trusted the wrong contractor and gave him too much power. In this deal gone bad, some very unexpected things happened. For example, my beautiful hardwood floor was stolen! I also chose an unscrupulous title company. I learned a lot of things from all of this, including that the valuation must be right in a fix 'n' flip. Needless to say, I don't fix 'n' flop now. I believe more in the buy-and-hold strategy. Even wholesaling can fall into this category. In buy-and-hold you can valuate "off" and hold the property till the numbers match.

I have also learned about a little thing called a "Subject To" Transaction. "Subject To" is a type of real estate transaction used to assign ownership rights in exchange for repayment of mortgage notes. During times like we are experiencing now when it's tough to get a line of credit from a bank (though I very rarely take this route), "Subject To" offers an alternative to traditional financing and allows the seller to get out from under his/her mortgage note. People facing foreclosure may be open to this type of transaction, because it can help them

avoid the foreclosure. With a "Subject To" the homeowner assigns ownership rights to a buyer, but the seller keeps the note in his/her name. The buyer assumes ownership and makes payments on the mortgage on behalf of the seller. When entering into this type of arrangement, it's best to consult with a real estate attorney to make sure you're doing things right. There's a lot more that goes into a "Subject To" deal, and I'm not a real estate attorney, so I won't go any further. If you are interested in this type of deal, there is good real estate investment training available. Or contact a real estate attorney who will help you with the process. I can say that it can be a very lucrative area of investing. Plus, you can help distressed homeowners. If you want to ask me about how to use "Subject To" in your deals, we can talk. Email me from my website at www.CashflowDiary.com. I help clients with all sorts of issues. One of the issues I hear about is how to get into making money with short sales. If you're interested in short sales you can make good money. It is similar to wholesaling, but there are differences.

What about foreclosure properties?

I get asked frequently if there is a place to find foreclosure properties. Yes! Absolutely! And it's a good market to get into. You might even be able to help a few people in the process. But that would be more during the pre-foreclosure period. That's what I was able to do in my first transaction. The woman I told you that I helped who said she needed $12K to get out of her situation. Remember her? I found the money through another investor (he had the money somewhere,

but at this stage I was too new to know to ask him). I quickly fixed the place up and put a renter in there. In this case, the woman's mortgage was far lower than what I knew I could get in rent, so it worked out for everyone. She avoided foreclosure and I gave a tenant a good home. In the process, I did my first really successful transaction and I still earn a passive income from that property! That's called a win-win-win.

As for foreclosure properties, there are a couple of places you can go online to find them. You can download an app or go to a website called www.redfin.com. You can also get a subscription to www.foreclosureradar.com. Now, when you do that, you need to start paying attention to the properties that are going to go to the foreclosure auction (or trustee sale). Pay attention to the tax deed auction that happens in each of the counties listed. The tax deed auction is going to be different per county. They all have different time frames and a different work for you to participate in the tax deeds. The reason I'm going through this is because at the end of the day what we're talking about right now is how you will acquire your inventory to sell. We're working on a helpful e-book about tax sales, so keep an eye out on my site for that. Download it for free when you see it!

At the end of the day you've got to have multiple ways of acquiring pre-foreclosure and foreclosure inventory. For one, you can find deals on foreclosure auctions. You're going to go to www.redfin.com and www.foreclosureradar.com to figure out when those are in each of those counties that you want to work in. Then you're going to go to the different county websites to learn when the tax deed auctions are going to be held in each of those counties. Next you're going to begin looking for pre-foreclosure lists in each of those counties.

Don't forget the pre-foreclosure list!

The pre-foreclosure list is known as the NOD (Notice of Default) list. You're going to get the NOD lists for each of those counties you're interested in. Then you have to market to that list. You can market any way you'd like. You can use direct mail. You can use yellow letters. You can use door-knocking. That's one of my personal favorites. It's the least efficient, but it's most effective because you have to take your time and literally knock on all those doors and talk to people. Talk about opportunity! You can solve problems in a big way and help people.

You have to do all the "horrible" marketing stuff you wish you could avoid. The NOD list is the same thing as your lead list. If you want to work in pre-foreclosures, you have to market to that list. A smart move would be to create a quick information-only website about short sales and pre-foreclosures. Short sales are a route that homeowners in pre-foreclosure use. That's because they don't know about you yet! Get out there and talk to them. Be their solution to a very painful problem.

Your message at networking events would be clear: "My name is [YOUR NAME], and I buy houses from people who have trouble making their mortgage payments." You're literally

going to say these words. As a wholesaler, you're going to tell people, "I'm a wholesaler. I buy properties at a discount. I sell properties at a discount. What kind of investing are you looking to do?"

You can find out from people at these events what kind of investing they are looking to do, because you still have to collect your buyers. That's still going to be something that happens, even in foreclosures. In that process, because you said you want to serve the retail market, you need to be aware that what you're really looking for in a buyer is someone who says, "I'm not looking."

You want their response to be, "I'm not actually looking to do investment. I'm looking for a place for myself." Or when you ask a question and they start answering your questions about what type of investing you're looking to do, you want to ask another question. "Is this property for yourself or is it for a renter that you're hoping to have?"

You need to know if are they looking for retail or are they looking for the turnkey stuff? You have to ask that question when you go to the networking affair, in your marketing materials or when they call you back (or however they contact you). This is what must happen or else you will not get the information that you need in order to put the deal together.

With the Notice of Trustee Sale, hopefully you're in the position by that point to help the seller (the person with the big problem) get under contract with you so that you have the ability to negotiate directly with the bank and go out and perform the short sale so that you can postpone the sale and, more importantly, get control of the property. You want the ability to negotiate directly.

Once you've negotiated the proper purchase price, the next person you're going to need in the short sale process is going to be what is called a "transactional funder." There are many transactional funders out there. This is someone who is willing to lend you private funds for three to seven days, just long enough for you to find a buyer.

When you go to networking groups, look for these transactional funders who can literally give you all the money that is necessary to purchase the property. They won't just give you the money. They'll take three to six points on the deal, plus charge about 10% interest. It is worth the amount you will pay when you find a buyer. You have to work fast though.

You need to develop what is traditionally called an investor profile sheet. You need to begin to create some sort of a database. I don't care if it's a whole bunch of Word docs or Excel sheets or whatever, but you need to be able to keep that information easily accessible so that you can recall the information at any time. You never know when that next buyer or seller will respond to your marketing efforts!

You have a goal. You need to get to a place where for any one house that you have under contract you also have at least five potential buyers. At least five! Anything less and you're likely

going to get stuck with the house. You don't want that! If you follow the steps here, believe it or not, it should take you maybe 30 days to get up and running in your real estate business, helping people with foreclosure problems. It depends on what marketing you use. If you just hit the streets and start going to networking groups, you can probably get something done faster, but you're going to have to start immediately. You need to talk to people and get their property profile together so that you understand what it is that you need to do.

Those are the physical steps you need to do right now. All of it is based upon the customers you want to serve. If you have questions about this process, I'm waiting for you online at www.CashflowDiary.com! You'll find a tab to the side of the home page that takes you directly to a place where you can leave your questions. You can also participate in my LIVE Deal Reviews each week at www.CashFlowDiary.TV. Sign up to receive email notifications about them. Now we need to get back to OPM and how to get people to let you use their money for your deals.

Getting OPM means you're gonna have to talk to people!

"OPM" is an abbreviation we in the investing community love. It stands for "Other People's Money." That's a wonderful thing when you are entrusted by investors to utilize their funds to buy properties and solve problems. However, you have to earn that trust, and that starts with conversations and

ASKING QUESTIONS. Oh, and your best listening skills. We touched on this topic in the last step, but now let's put it to practice. First, let's walk through a reason why you would want to endeavor getting other people involved in your deals.

The short answer is that you can achieve more if you involve others in your vision and can make them see that being part of your vision is the answer to their problem. Second, if you can make monthly income from the properties and the investors won't just make their money back but also a nice profit over time, what would be your hold up on speaking with people about coming on board with your vision?

Do the math with me here. Say I find a property that will make an excellent rental if only I rehab it. Now let's say that I need $12K to make the rental property actually rentable. The property sat unsellable and therefore unrentable for a long time because no one had the vision of what it would take to make it rentable. If I don't have the money to do the rehab, I would have to ask around to see who might be able to put that money up. (In this example, let's say the seller has agreed to let me have the property under a set of terms that we have both agreed to.) Do I look for ONE person who has $12K or do I ask myself all the people I might know who have a little money? Both!

So now I start having the conversation with different people. I ask them if they would like $100 a month in passive income. Their ears perk up. Who wouldn't like $100? Suddenly they are open to the conversation. I commence in laying out my

vision. I can make sure they get their money back plus passive income for a very long time. Maybe it's not $100. Maybe it's less or maybe it's more, because just maybe I am speaking with a single individual who would back my vision with his $12K. In my world, this happens all the time and with larger and larger numbers in larger and larger deals. I learned how to speak with different types of investors and to organize people with complimentary skills. I first had to be willing to take the risk of talking to people. Isn't it worth the risk if you know or are at least willing to believe you can get other people to help you reach your vision and to help them, too? Your job as a real estate investor is to find those who understand this concept.

You might think it would be a risk, but not really. Besides, we are ALL risk-takers.

Think about it. Every time we get behind the wheel of our vehicle, we take a risk. We cross the street; we take a risk. We eat food from a buffet line; we take a risk. You get the idea. On the scheme of things, what risk is there really in opening a conversation with other people about your vision?

One thing that stops us from entering the real estate investing arena is that we think asking for money from others is a big deal. It's not. It's only new to us. You make a choice to be afraid and then you let that fear stop you. (I told you I'd be visiting this topic a lot, and there's a reason. I want you to put your fears aside. They aren't helping you move forward in your life.) Why not instead of saying you are "fearful" say that you are "excited"? Tony Robbins, a motivational speaker and life trainer I respect a whole lot, has people do an exercise in simply replacing negative words with more positive words. That simple exercise does wonders for the brain. It can make you move forward with your dreams. If you CHOOSE to do your first real estate transaction it will change your life and your mindset forever. I know. It happened to me!

Maybe thinking about asking to use other people's money will be less scary to you if I get you to think a little differently. Remember the pen conversation earlier in this book? If I were to ask you if I can use your pen for a minute, would you let me? Have you ever asked someone to use his/her pen? Strangers? Did you get the pen because you made it clear that you didn't just need the pen, but you needed it so you could write a few notes and you didn't have your own pen? They have a pen; you need a pen; they lend you their pen. When you are done with it you hand it back. This is the same theory of asking people if you can use their money for a down payment on a property or to rehab a property. Once they understand the goal because you have clearly defined it and they see your vision and they understand that you will be sending them checks (and you've asked them when they'd like you to stop and they've said never), they might just let you use their money. It's called INVESTING. Banks lend. Investors invest and get returns.

So… what's REALLY stopping you?

It's not just fear that holds you back. There is also an educational challenge you face before taking your first steps into real estate. We've all been taught in school to recognize only ONE opportunity. Yep, it's the J-O-B. "They" want us to have a job, whoever "they" are. (They sure seem to have a lot of say in our lives. Don't let them.) As I more than mentioned in Step One, there's more to life and earning a living than collecting a paycheck. There are so many ways to earn a good living, especially today where there are opportunities all around us! You just have to see the opportunities and take action. It is that simple. If you can't do it alone, you can certainly do it with others.

When I did my first transaction in real estate, I felt great. Then I did another and another in short time. People called me "lucky." No, I'm not. I see opportunity everywhere and then I act. I DO IT. You know what LUCK is anyway?

Laboring

Under

Correct

Knowledge for better results!
+
Willingness to take actions at the speed of instruction.

So, yeah, maybe I AM lucky! What I am is a provider of solutions in the real estate investing world and, for me, participating in real estate is a whole lot of fun! I couldn't imagine doing anything else right now. I may add a business or two, but it's still going to have something to do with real estate. I enjoy what I do too much! I get a kick out of providing solutions.

Here's a tip. We can all be solution-providers if we just get out of our own way. Like the old saying goes, it's amazing what can be achieved when you don't care who gets the credit. Think in a team mentality. YOU can't do anything in real estate (or likely any other area of your life) alone. It takes a team. Look at basketball, a sport that is near and dear to my heart. Every player is important, but so are the other "team members." The water boy is necessary, the towel person is necessary, the coaches are necessary, and the fans are necessary. Everyone contributes. Taking this approach a bit higher, you know that even Jesus had a team. He knew he couldn't accomplish his goals alone. He gathered 12 apostles who helped him.

I learned early on that I could do "it" alone or I could do more things faster by building a team I can trust. Now anything and any deal is possible! At the time of this writing we (notice I didn't say I) just closed on a 182-unit apartment complex. You think I could have done that without the support and expertise of other individuals? Maybe, but it would have taken longer and I might have made mistakes that could have stopped the deal. Later in the book, I've included a step on building your

team and what types of people you need to include in it. I learned the hard way. Let me make it easier for you!

Right now, here's what I want to get across to you. I don't need to understand how to do "it" all. I can ask for help. I'm not so good at doing paperwork. So? I let others do it that are good at it. Doing the paperwork is not the best use of my time. It is not my strength. I also don't micro manage the members of my team. I ask them for their help, we agree on the job and then I let them do their job again and again and again. People can be trusted and they will do well. This is a topic I cover later in the book, too.

Everyone is good at something. For example, I love photography. Visit my Facebook page at www.facebook.com/cashflowdiary. I share my photos online and I always carry a camera. It's a creative release. I can take pictures of houses, too. You'll see before-and-after shots in this book. Guess who the photographer was? Me! And I loved every minute of taking those pictures to share with you. One might wonder why I devote any time to photography. Hey, it's something I enjoy. It inspires me. We all need inspiration and an outlet for stresses, right?

Back to assessing your investors…

A few paragraphs back, I told you that I group investor types. You might wonder what I mean by that. It boils down to understanding your investor's identity. That is actually a two-sided fence. On one side, you have to understand YOUR identity in that you need to know what types of deals you are best suited to manage. On the other side are the people who are going to help you in those deals; your investors.

I teach a class on investor identity, so the class participants can decide what types of investments they are best suited to manage. I am familiar with apartment buildings. I'm an Army brat. I've lived in apartments. I understand apartment dwellers. I love buying apartment buildings, fixing them up (which as you will see in my pictures can be a huge undertaking) and then creating clean, safe, affordable housing for people who might not otherwise get to live in a decent dwelling. Others may understand commercial properties. This is an area of real estate investing that I'm getting into in bigger and bigger ways. Remember that I said I see real estate everywhere I look and that I even think about owning a jail. Hey, that's a big commercial property, right?

Beyond buying and selling properties, and beyond providing clean, safe, affordable housing, there's something else my vision includes that I cannot do on my own. As part of MY investor identity, I want to plant the seed with kids at events I host for that purpose, so that the kids at the events can understand that they can achieve what I have achieved… no matter where they come from and no matter what financial condition their families find themselves in. (I'll tell you more about my Cashflow Camps for Kids and the Basketball Camp later. Or you can visit my website at www.CashflowDiary. com for more on that at this very minute.) I want these kids to become problem-solvers as opposed to becoming a problem for society.

You will note that I use the phrase "I became a problem-solver" throughout this book. Why do I hammer this point home? If you want to raise capital you will become a problem-solver, too. You will figure out your investor identity and then you will begin spreading your simple message about your vision and what you need from people. You will determine their investor type... their identity. And then you will be successful.

My message at networking events is simple. I shared it with you earlier, but I don't want you to have to flip back through the pages to find it. When I attend events where I know there are active real estate investors in the room (others who also buy and sell property and those who will help me reach my vision) I make one simple statement:

"Hi, my name is J. Massey. I buy real estate at a discount and I sell real estate at a discount. If you have property, even if they have problems, give me a call."

This simple statement continues to lead me to open conversations. One of the first times this happened, I was at a networking event and I delivered my message. That led to a conversation with a woman investor at an event who was upside down. (No, she wasn't standing on her head, though that would have been an interesting story.) We chatted a bit about her "problem" and I came up with a solution. I could help her get out of that property. It would cost about $12K. (Now you know where that $12K number came from in my last example.) We struck a verbal agreement and I had a mission: to get the $12K. That was the beginning for me, and it was thrilling!

Next, I went to other people and found the money needed to fix her problem. Getting there meant I would just have conversations about the "problem" with the property and what it would take to fix it, and then how I would give a return on investment. Another investor had $12,000. Excellent! He agreed to put it to use for my vision. I went back to the woman and told her I could solve her problem, but I needed a contract. I did not know how to do this part, but I learned quickly. Then I had someone teach me about other parts, like escrow. What's that, I thought? I learned what it was. The escrow company asked me about closing. What's that? I learned about closing, too. I got the deed for the home with none of my own money. I fixed the woman's problem. Then I had a house. At that point I remember thinking this is kind of strange. I was literally looking over my shoulder. I thought, "Is this going to be taken away?" The answer is no. There is a reason the deal worked and there is a reason why I was worried that someone was going to squash it. It has to do with my upbringing.

Our childhood can haunt us. Dump the ghosts!

Like you, I was raised under a certain set of ideals. And perhaps like you (like our entire society) I was told that I cannot do A, B and C. It's just not the way things are done. I don't blame my parents for thinking this way, and I've proven

them wrong (in a very nice way). It is how they were raised that made them think that way. I am not passing that way of thinking to my offspring.

Begging your pardon here, but if you were to see me, you would quickly realize that I am clearly a tall black man. Looking at me without knowing who I am, you might make a few assumptions. That's incorrect thinking. I don't care what race, gender, culture, religion or even age you happen to be, you cannot let ASSUMPTIONS hold you back from success in anything! I don't want to hear it. Do not let any of those monikers hold you back from success. Why on earth would you let anything hold you back if you know there is a better life waiting?

My family and old friends sure don't tell me I can't do something now. They have seen me go from broke to going for broke in all that I do! (Where does that term come from? Who wants to really "go for broke"? Wouldn't it be better to say "go for wealth and prosperity"?) But I'm not alone. We as individuals always hear that we have to do things in a specific way or things just can't be done this way or that way. It's simply not true. My wife and I have learned over the past few years that there are all sorts of ways to do things in life, especially when it comes to real estate investing. Together we have stepped through some very hard times. Now we are in celebration mode every day. Why? Because we changed our mindset to allow ourselves to be open to opportunities in real estate. We can look back and think that WE did all of this, having gone through all of the pain that we did, and we are here at a successful point in our lives that we created. What if we had listened to the nay-sayers?

I live in Orange County, California. As a black man, I'm not exactly the typical Orange County resident. I was not raised in this environment. As a young man I would never have thought living here was possible, but here I am. I see this same attitude when working with basketball players. White, black or whatever, they look at my lack of credentials while at the same time they listen to some financial planner or their managers about how to handle their money. These "financial planning" professionals would have the players put their money in a bank, mutual fund or in a low-interest-bearing account and they would not have them invest in real estate, something that will bring them certain returns over the years. I find it funny that the players would take the advice of a financial planner before taking advice about real estate investing from someone who has made a lot of money through this means because I don't have certain letters following my name or a license hanging on my wall. I said it before and I'll say it again… It takes more time to become a hairstylist than to become a financial planner. It takes very little time to become licensed as a financial planner. Ninety days! That's right… 90. But that's fine. Take the advice of the "learned" professionals. I'll be over here investing in another apartment building and making extremely good money from my investments not just for me but for everyone involved. Oh, and I'll be creating some good in this world by providing clean, safe, affordable housing. Whether the basketball or football players join in my vision or not doesn't matter. It won't affect my motivation.

Stay motivated, no matter what.

People ask me about my motivation. It's pretty easy, really. I said it before and I'll say it again. I have to feed my family. I will never lose sight of this fact, and there was a point where I couldn't really feed my family very well. I remember what it felt like to have to go to my mother and father to ask for help and to be refused. They weren't in a position to help me. I had to work through this financial crisis myself, and I had to turn my own life around my own way. I thank God every day for the life I lead as a real estate investor (and photographer). I can now focus on creating a legacy plan for my children. I don't think people understand how important leaving a legacy really is.

Have you ever heard of the family name Vanderbilt? No. Why? Because that family didn't plan well for the future of their money. They left no legacy; they had no legacy plan in place. That's not an example I want to follow. I want my children to know that they can do what I did, to achieve what I have. I show them that through their actions they can change their lives. These actions shouldn't involve buying a bunch of stuff none of us really need. There is a famous quote I like a lot about family by Charles R. Swindoll that says:

> *"A family is a place where principles are hammered and honed on the anvil of everyday living."*

In my home, we take this to heart. We don't believe in buying bling. It costs money. In my family, if my kids want something, and they come to me to ask for it, my response is always the same. They can have what they want. All they have to do is come up with a product or service to sell to create the money to buy what they want. My oldest daughter gets this implicitly. I mentioned this earlier, but I am really proud of her for being a teenager who has created her own crochet products to sell. I have nothing to do with it. She sees a lifestyle she wants and she is working toward it. She has seen both her parents work up from zero to have and to be able to share with the world what they have accomplished. We are setting a great example for her and for our other children.

What type of lifestyle do you want to lead?

I guess you can call me a "lifestyle coach" for lack of better words. I run everything through a virtual office, and I'm not tied to any one geographic location, state or even continent. I don't view my success in financial terms only. Success is literally being able to do what one wants to do where he wants to do it. It's a conscious choice of taking action with intent. If I wanted to accomplish X, Y and Z, I cannot get there by sitting around watching TV or playing video games. (Though I really enjoy playing video games!) There are action steps I must take. I have to take those steps with integrity and do what I say I will do when I say I will do it. Being successful is the easy part. Being a man of integrity is harder.

Some may look at my life and see a guy who has reached his goals. What could possibly be next? Let me share a secret

90

with you. Yes, I reached my first goals, but the goal post is always changing. Yours will, too, and pushing out your goals to be bigger and bigger benefits you in a big way! Here's what I mean. In life, we may start out with one set of goals. They might be small or attainable in our minds. But what happens when we reach them? Do we just say, "Okay. That's done. Whew!" Do we just hang up our track shoes and stop running? I don't think so. We readjust the goal line. We push it further out with bigger goals, and we keep doing that until… I don't know. Maybe never.

I took a time out from working toward new goals. You know what happened? Nothing. It was boring. Could I have stopped at being the owner of a couple of hundred properties and receiving a very good amount of monthly passive income from my rentals? Sure, but it wasn't fulfilling. So, I started traveling and speaking at events, and that wasn't wholly satisfying either. I missed my wife and kids. I hung out alone. That's not who I am. I learned something about myself. I am a doer. I need to keep moving forward. I will always push the goals out. I attain one and I then add another, larger goal. My vision is HUGE! I want yours to be huge. Start small, sure, but keep going. Keep moving the goals outward. In the following graphics you will understand how pain is actually a motivating force. Pain will get you moving toward your goals because you don't want to experience the pain any longer. And once you reach your first goal, it's time to push it out!

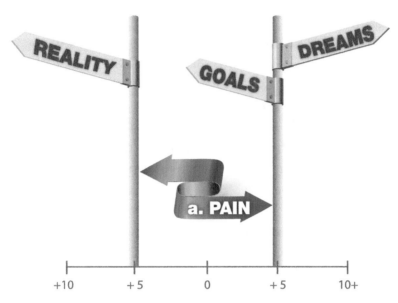

A. We start out with our Reality and our Dreams/Goals.
They are too close to experience enough pain to take action.

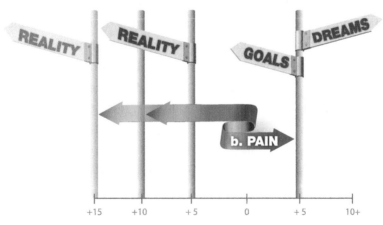

B. When something shifts in our REALITY and the pain divide widens, we
tend to step more quickly to action to make positive change in our lives.

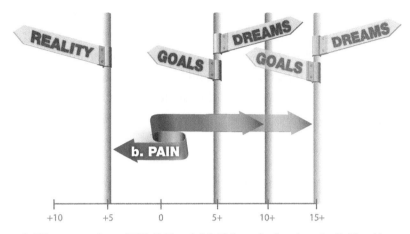

C. *When we push our DREAMS and GOALS out further the pain divide widens and we have to take a series of action steps to reach those new goals. The secret is to keep pushing the goals out to bigger and bigger dreams!*

My largest vision includes working more with Hope Worldwide. If you want to learn about this organization, visit them at www.hopeww.org. Following is their mission statement, so you can understand why I want to become more involved with this group:

> **HOPE worldwide is an international charity that changes lives by harnessing the compassion and commitment of dedicated staff and volunteers to deliver sustainable, high-impact, community-based services to the poor and needy.**

I want to work with this organization to help them develop a system to create more income for their needs. Hope Worldwide is a good organization, but they don't have the help they need right now, so I will fill that slot. If it's got to be… it's going to be me! That's my personal philosophy and

93

it keeps pushing me forward. If a hospital needs to be built, who is going to build it if not me? If hungry people are going to be fed and educated so they can achieve a better life, who is going to do it if not me? If we all had this attitude, if we all thought "if not me" wouldn't the world be a better place? We could all be people of influence if we choose to be. Hey, I'm juss sayin'.

I want even more freedom in my life to have family reunions and to have more time to pursue my photography. I want to provide a lot more value in this world. My goal, and people sometimes think I'm nuts, is to have 1,000 free and clear units of real estate and 1,000,000 square feet (92.900 square meters for me European friends) of commercial space. And I want to create jobs domestically and in far-away lands like Belize, one of the most beautiful places I have ever experienced. I am well on my way to these goals. I won't quit.

At the end of the day it hurts me to know that mothers and fathers quit. They give up because they have been told they cannot or that they don't fit the mold of a successful person. Hey, I understand, but my wife and I came from a dark place. We didn't fit the mold either, but I'm writing this book. We set goals and we achieved them. If we can achieve so much in just six years, you have to understand that means you can, they can, we all can achieve what we want.

Your story is not over!

I want people to live their lives. I want you to know that no matter what has happened in your life that your story is not over. You get to shape your own character. You get to choose to live with integrity. Everything changes when you change your approach to your life. Let me get back to my early days for just a minute to drive this point home.

I've lived through a lot of trauma and drama. You now know that my home was foreclosed and I squatted in that property for a spell. I learned very quickly that I had to adapt to the new way of thinking or I would die. I was driven to be successful in real estate investing. But I didn't get out unscathed. When we moved to a rental that was only 1,100 square feet and I had three children and a wife, it might shock you to know that I was actually afraid to move again later when we were on our feet and could afford something much larger. I had property. I was a landlord, and I was already working toward my goal of owning 1,000 units of real estate. Yet I was afraid to find a larger home and to move. I was afraid that somehow all of this good fortune and all of my hard work would be taken away from me. I had to change my thinking… again. And I did. I'm hoping by your reading my words that you can change your life, too, if that is what you really want to do. But you have to want it enough to work hard for it. You have to have a sense of urgency about changing your life and taking a new path that you can sink your teeth into. Otherwise it's just a wish.

So you WISH you could get into wholesaling?

I don't want to leave this step without giving you a bit more tutoring on how wholesaling works. Maybe wholesaling fits your investor identity. This will help you figure that part out. Wholesaling is simply a way to acquire real estate using none of your own money or credit. I am not going to go into it fully here, because you can become a Premium Member of www.CashflowDiary.com and take my Wholesaling Training Course. This comes with a special workbook intended to complement your training. The workbook includes questions to guide you through the content and wholesaling process.

As a wholesaler, you acquire the property at a discount and you sell it at a discount. This is how I started becoming successful in real-estate investing. I suggest that you begin with single-family houses. You can move into bigger deals after you get good at wholesaling single-family homes.

In wholesaling, there are two basic concepts you have to understand. There is a difference between owning something and controlling something. Once you understand this part, wholesaling can work well for you. That is one of the first concepts that I was trained in that helped me to understand how to do a wholesale transaction. Basically, with a wholesale transaction you are acquiring CONTROL of a property; you are not necessarily purchasing that property. You are acquiring control of the property in such a way that gives you the ability to then sell the control.

Step one is to acquire the control; step two is to sell the control. Once you have sold control you are done with the deal. Understanding how to do this is the key to success in wholesaling. You also have to understand the value of a property and how different buyers attach different types of value to that property. For example, inside the wholesaling world you have three basic types of customers (buyers):

1) **Retail customer** – These buyers see value in holding onto the property long term and want to live in it.
2) **Wholesale customer** – These buyers are typically looking to fix and then flip the property, which means that they are looking to ADD value to it so they can make a good profit.
3) **Turnkey (buy and hold) customer** – These buyers are looking for additional cash flow that they intend to create by doing some minor (or perhaps major, like adding a laundry room or day care center) improvements if needed to the property and then renting it out.

Once you understand each of these buyer types, you'll know how to value the deal and sell your control over that particular piece of property to someone else.

Wholesaling requires that you understand at least a basic contract between parties, the buyer and the seller. You may be the buyer or you may find a buyer. In fact, you are brokering a deal as a principal, unless you intend to buy the property at a discount to create a rental property. Regardless, you should get acquainted with something called a Master Lease. If I just lost you or if you're screaming into the pages of this book right now about how you don't know anything about leases or contracts, calm down. Remember that you don't have to know everything. There are people for that. Besides, I learned how to do basic contracts, which means you can learn, too.

A Master Lease is a very simple strategy that you can use to control a building without taking ownership. That's the key. You're going to use a contract that gives you the ability to control the use of the building without actually owning the building. Say you have a five-, ten- or 15-unit apartment building or perhaps a commercial space. The Master Lease works well for that. You could lease all of the spaces from the owner at a discounted rate and what the owner receives is at least a guaranteed amount of rent. He/she knows that a certain amount of rent will come in monthly. Your job as a wholesaler is to then turn around and sublease each of those spaces differently and in a way that earns profit. That's what a Master Lease does really well. This doesn't calculate into the deal any common area maintenance charges (which are fees charged for the upkeep and maintenance of the building) and that gets into the minutia of the deal that you as a beginner might not be ready for. Taxes and insurance could be a part of the common area maintenance, too. It is how you write the deal that will dictate who is actually responsible for those fees, as in the landlord (you) or the tenant.

Because this is not a real estate investing training course, that's as far as I'm going to go here. This book is about the steps I

took and continue taking in real estate and steps you will need to take to be successful. If you've been through real estate investment training, you might be more concerned about how to generate leads than actually writing an offer (which is only an invitation to chat) or writing up the contracts. You might be ready to write offers (formally referred to as a "Residential Purchase Agreement," the "Residential Purchase Contract," the "REPSI" or even the "SP"), but you don't know how to get leads. I want to spend more time on that subject right now.

Getting leads: My exact strategy!

Getting leads is the only path to raising private capital. That's a golden rule. Aside from playing the Cashflow game, which is my absolute best way to get in front of like-minded people, you need to do a few things. For example, get people to sit down with you one-on-one to chat. You might say, "That sounds scary, J." I assure you, it's not. It's necessary. It shows that you actually care enough about the people you're approaching to learn more about them, have a cup a coffee with them (they buy their own coffee and Starbucks will give an ice water for free) and provide solutions to their problems. How else are you going to achieve this function?

Unless you have money for high-dollar and ongoing marketing and advertising, you're going to have to get in front of people through your own devices. As you know, I walked the streets putting message cards on cars. Yes, it worked. In fact, as I started combining more and more strategies and it worked too well. It was very hard to keep up and soon five months had passed without my following up with many of the leads. I had to find a more efficient strategy. I began attending networking events that were centered around business and investing. I wanted to be in a room with other real estate investors and interested others.

I like going to events like this when I'm looking for something in particular. That way, I can go in with a specific message. I use meetup.com to find events and sometimes BNI (Business Networking International) and LeTip. You've probably heard of these groups. You don't have to become a member of BNI and LeTip to give your message, but you do need to go as someone's guest. I like meetups because there are a lot of different types of gatherings. There may be an entry fee of about $25, but it's totally worth it.

When at an event, you're waiting for THE question, "So, what do you do?" How you answer this question can be a turn off or a turn on for the listener. You have very few seconds in which to convey your message and capture their interest. Remember that my elevator pitch is simple. So is the scripting for the in-person back-and-forths. It is really a formula. Here is what that looks like:

It is the word (I) followed by (a descriptor of what you are) followed by (an action verb in a phrase), in (target market), followed by (how-to benefit) so they can (benefit).

For example, "I am a real estate investor who buys properties at a discount and sells them at a discount to create passive

income for my investors, which allows them more freedom in their lives."

According to your audience you will change that script to fit their needs so you can help different people solve different problems. Say, for example, you're chatting with someone at an event, and both of you are there because you have a shared interest in real estate investing. That tells you the person might be looking for solutions to a problem. Great! Chat and learn more. Here is where you call into effect your communication and listening skills, a truly lost art form! In short time the person expresses that he/she will never be able to retire. Bingo! There it is. That person's pain point. Now you know how you can solve that person's problem.

ME: "I help people use their retirement plans to invest in real estate, which brings them passive income so they can stop worrying about having enough money to retire."

You just got the person's full attention. Maybe you can help them with their problem, they think. What's cool about this is when you state certain benefits, people can remember the benefits. Even if the person you're chatting with isn't ready to move forward with you, they will remember what you said. When they run into someone who says something like, "Oh, you know, I'm concerned about having enough money for retirement," chances are that the person you spoke to at the event will remember you or the benefits of what you shared with them. The next thing that happens is a referral, because the person you spoke with at the event is now telling his/

her friend, "I just met a guy/gal who was talking about that and he/she was telling me how he/she can make sure that you never run out of money." This referral came because you kept your message short and because you TARGETED your market (the individual's point of concern), because you live in integrity and you can deliver on what you say you can deliver.

You might have 15 or 20 variations on that script. It is an excellent exercise to grab a sheet of paper and jot down 15 action messages for different situations that you can use later. If you're going to be a successful real estate investor, you need to embrace the art of simple messaging and make it adaptable to the different investors (remember the investor identity) you will run into at functions. Create a script for the retirement plan investor, the person who has just a little bit of money but is interested in investing, for the investor who has a few thousand dollars to invest, the elderly investor and for people who might want to actually do what you do. Regardless of who you are talking to about investing, when the message is delivered to a room of investors you have a good chance of creating leads.

I thought about sharing with you here information from one of my Cash Flow Diary podcasts (in iTunes) to illustrate the process of gathering solid leads. This, of course, follows your initial meetings at real estate investing and other networking events and your online interactions or however you first meet people you want to help and work with. (Even the cherished Cashflow game encounters.) This is in episode 18, the podcast titled "How to Find Leads Using Little or No Money." (I could

have easily titled this section "Scripting for Real Estate Leads 101.") Instead of telling you all about what I say in the podcast episode, it's better that I just send you to it so you can take a listen. Don't stop there. Listen to all of the podcasts. They don't cost you a dime, so why wouldn't you listen to them? To tease you just a little, this episode of the podcast talks about what you do once you've piqued someone's interest in real estate investing. Here's a hint: Invite them to meet you for coffee. This is a great opportunity for you to answer their questions and ask a lot of questions yourself. In the episode, I cover the importance of having a calendar in your phone and how to use it to schedule appointments on the spot at events. I want you to listen to this episode, because it puts you further onto your path of earning money from your investments and helping others earn good money, too. Once you've gotten good at finding leads, you'll need a good system and script. Lucky for you I happen to have one!

The life of a lead: Getting people to call you back.

So you listened to episodes in both my Cash Flow Diary and Cash Flow Diary Daily podcasts, and you've read everything you can about getting leads. You took the bull by the horns, put your running shoes on and got the leads. Now what? You've called the leads and nothing happened. You called more. Nothing. You're getting discouraged. Hey, like the saying goes, you know the definition of insanity? Doing the same things over and over and expecting different results. It's time to think differently and do differently.

Are you tired of never having your phone calls returned? Looking for a foolproof way of making sure that people call you back? If you're like me, you've noticed that you can't exactly sell a product to a voice message. You actually need to talk to a person. So here's the concept. Talk to people! Yeah, I know. Sounds simple. Well, it is. Leverage the fact that we as humans are naturally curious.

Here's what you're going to do. The next time you have to leave a message because the lead didn't pick up your call, this is the message I want you to leave. This is EXACTLY what I want you to say, and nothing more. Okay? Okay.

At the sound of the beep, you are going to say, "'Hi, [NAME OF LEAD]. This is [YOUR NAME]. It's about [DAY], [TIME]. My phone number is [YOUR NUMBER]. I just wanted to make sure that you got the information about…" Then hang up.

That's right. I am telling you to end the call mid-sentence. Now, let's think about that for a second. Why would I tell you to do that? Because in this day and age, how often has a call been disconnected while leaving a voice mail? This is especially true of cell phones! And if this has ever happened to you, if you've dropped a call or someone on the other end drops the call what happens? That's right. Someone's going to call back. So what do you think the person on the other end of your "dropped call" is likely to assume? They're likely to assume that the call was dropped. But you left your name. You left your phone number, the date and the time. That's all you

104

need to leave. What happens next? They call you back. Give it a try and see what happens.

I've taught this technique at many of my events. The best in the crowd will try the technique during a lunch or bathroom break with people and prospects they haven't heard from in a long time. They try it once and that person calls back during another break because he/she is curious about what's going on and what happened. The call got disconnected. OMG! Now what? Here's the point. You aren't calling to bug people. You just want to talk to them so that you can find out what it is that they want so that you can serve them. And we can't serve them unless they talk to us. (Remember that you got their information because they are interested in some aspect of real estate.) You're getting nowhere fast if you don't actually speak to them. You're making a mistake not to speak to them, and you're losing out on opportunities by not speaking to them. You know what you're doing then? Losing money.

In the next step, I'll share with you ways to NOT lose money. In real estate, there are plenty of ways to lose money. I know. I've had some amazing experiences that lost me money in ways I'd never dreamed possible. By reading my stories, I hope to help you avoid the same pitfalls and keep more green in your jeans!

STEP THREE

Don't Lose Money

"Successful people ask better questions and, as a result, they get better answers." Tony Robbins

Before I share with you ways to lose money, let's recap what we learned in the last section. If you want to attain private capital from investors for your real estate deals, the best thing you can do is ASK QUESTIONS and then – and this is really important – LISTEN! Don't have your own agenda playing in your head while other people are speaking. Actually LISTEN with your full attention. Only then can you 1) define the problem they are having and 2) provide a solution that would make them want to work with you.

Here's something I didn't mention in the last section, and it's important. When raising private capital, you must be "multi-lingual." No, I'm not saying you have to speak many different languages, but rather you have to be well-versed in Investor-

Speak, CFO-Speak, CEO-Speak, Customer-Speak and so on. You have to understand what role the person plays in business and in life before you can speak to them in their "language." The perspective of a CFO (protector of money) will be different from other decision-makers in a group. The perspective of the guy who has $2M to invest with you in a large project will be different from the people who have a few thousand dollars to invest. The attorney uses a different language than the banker, and they all speak a different language than the homeowner.

While we're on the topic of language and words, have you considered your words and how they play into your own expectations? I'm talking about those expectations you set for yourself. For example, here's a powerful conversation-changer. It's the word YET. Add it to your vocabulary, especially when you're talking in terms of things that you want to obtain. Stick with me on this and then give it a try.

Often we'll say, "I've never done that." What we should say is, "I have yet to do that." Or maybe, "I haven't done that yet." Or how about, "I would like to do that one day." The way we phrase our words becomes our subliminal messaging that begins to build muscles in our minds that opens possibilities. All this by adding one simple word. YET!

In one of my quick videos that you'll find on my site I give an example. Consider two friends in a room. They're talking about the Super Bowl. One friend asks, "Hey, have you ever been to the Super Bowl?" The other friend responds, "No, I've never been." That just ended the conversation, didn't it?

There isn't much to be discussed after that. What if instead the friend responded with, "No, I haven't been YET." That sets up a bit of curiosity in the mind of the other person. He wants to learn more. He may ask, "Well, what do you mean by yet?" Or, "Were you planning on going?" Or, better still, "Would you like to go with me?" Just by adding that magic little word, a whole new world of possibilities now exists for these two individuals! Ah… language.

As an investor in real estate you need to understand all languages and use your best communication skills to effectively work with buyers, sellers and other investors. Questions are imperative to this process, but here's the deal… I can teach you everything I know as a real estate investor, but that is not going to stop you from losing money. You are always going to be learning and earning. Some of the lessons are hard. Some will cost you money. That is a promise, but don't let that idea stop you from getting into the game. Whatever you spend is your cost of learning. Do not look at it as money lost. (What would you pay an educational institution for the type of learning experience you will have on the street as you actively invest in real estate?)

If you are making investments you aim to earn returns on your investments, right? Some people quit when they have a bad first experience. Don't be one of those people. Wisdom only comes with mistakes. First you gain the knowledge, then you put that knowledge into action, which gains you real-world experience, and through the very real process you gain wisdom.

Don't take money from the wrong people.

Every person I've ever met that is worth his/her salt as a real estate investor has lost money. One way they've done so is by taking money from the wrong people. You read correctly. Yes, there is such a thing as accepting investment dollars from the wrong individuals… or investor type. That has happened to me and it will happen to you. That's almost a guarantee. I say "almost" because maybe you will be that one exception.

If you are not willing to make the mistakes or if you play small, you won't get to the level of success as a real estate investor that you crave. Did you know it's actually more challenging to make good cash flow investing in just three homes compared to owning 20 houses? When you get to 20 dwellings you see a huge shift in lifestyle, especially if a few of the dwellings are multi-family homes or, better yet, apartment buildings. What I'm saying is that the number of investments makes the difference. If that is an overwhelming thought, take a deep breath. Just like anything else in life, this will happen over time. Not tomorrow. Not today. Rather over time and as you develop your skills as a real estate investor.

Don't freak out about mistakes.

If someone had told me six years ago that I'd be buying apartment buildings and raising capital for international investments, it would have overwhelmed me. This became my goal after I learned my way around the single-family homes, then multi-family homes and then small apartment buildings

and now larger and larger apartment complexes, and finally commercial real estate. With the larger commercial deals came larger goals. And don't think I haven't had "failure events" along the way. Like I said, every single real estate investor I know who has achieved success has had lofty "failure events." So what? They didn't let these events stop them from moving forward with their plans.

I like to look at failure events like this… It's just a sentence in a paragraph in a story. The great thing is that you get to write the next sentence! It's no big deal. Failures and mistakes are a part of life. Think about it this way. Once you've had a magnificent failure event, you can strike it off your list. You feared it. The event happened. You faced it. You lived through it. Now it's done. Embrace it. Fail forward. Fail often. Make more deals faster! Yes, I said faster.

There are plenty of opportunities just waiting for you to find them in real estate. That means once you understand the process of putting buyers and sellers together (in the case of wholesaling) or finding a dwelling that would make an excellent rental property (buy-and-hold) and so on, your confidence will grow, which allows you to be bold and find more deals. Do them faster and faster. As I mentioned earlier, when I first started out I did 11 deals in one week. It was thrilling! I felt so exhilarated that I couldn't wait to do more deals and more and … well, you get the picture. Now I'm doing multiple deals simultaneously. While the number of transactions is lower, the value and impact of each transaction is now much more. And, for the record, it still thrills me!

You might ask me whether one state is better than another for finding deals. I get this question all the time. Admittedly, because the costs of properties are a lot higher in California, Hawaii and New York, it makes sense that there are "fewer opportunities" because the price of entry into the market is greater. This doesn't mean you can't participate in real estate investing in these states. It simply means you should look at the other 47 states where real estate in all forms may be less expensive. Do deals in states other than where you live. Again, do more deals faster than slower. If you do several deals over a three-month period, you'll have about six times the experience as someone who only does one or two deals in the same amount of time. Which model is more beneficial to you in helping you reach your personal and financial goals?

Let's do a little math to prove my point. In this case, we are looking at rental properties. Say you close on a single-family home and after expenses you will earn $400 a month in passive income (because the rent exceeds by that amount ALL of the expenses). Cool, but that's just $400 a month. Now you quickly make another offer and close a deal on another single-family home and you seal the deal so that you will earn $300 in passive income. Now you're up to $700 a month AFTER EXPENSES. Cool. Now you have more confidence and you quickly do three more deals. For the sake of argument, these are two four-unit dwellings and an eight-unit dwelling. You do some rehabbing and you covered the costs of that part and the down payment using OPM. Very cool. You structure a deal to pay back investors over time – and notice I didn't say to start right away, because you can structure that plan in ways

that suit both you and the investors. (We will cover that in the P.A.Q. section to come.)

Let's say that the units have residents fairly quickly and because you did a nice job on the rehab you are at full occupancy. Nice! For the sake of fast math, let's say that the renters each pay $600 a month. For those multi-family dwellings, you will gain $9,600 a month. Let's not talk about expenses right now. Focus in on the income. The $9,600 + $700 in passive income equals $10,300 per month. Excited yet? Understand the need to make more deals quickly vs. sitting back between deals? Doesn't this make sense? In my first year I was pulling six figures in income. Why is that? You got it. More deals faster™.

Choose the right location, location, location…

Where you make deals matters. If you live in California, you can certainly do deals in California. Remember that I have rental property in California. I live in California, but I make a lot of my deals in Tennessee, Colorado and other states. Think about this… If you can do only one deal in California yet can do several in say Memphis, doesn't it make more sense to do the several deals in Memphis? I choose Memphis in this example, because I invest in real estate there. Why? Because I know the area. Yes, I live and work in southern California, but I do a heck of a lot of deals in Tennessee because I have a passion for Memphis. Maybe yours is on the outskirts of Dallas or Houston. Power to you! Texas offers a lot of real estate opportunities. The job market has continued to be strong there even while job markets in other states slump. People flock to Texas to follow the job market. And what do they need once they arrive? That's right. A place to live, lay and play. (The "work" and "play" aspects are covered by someone else, but you could give them the housing to cover the "live" and "lay" needs.)

How do you accomplish that when you don't live in Texas? Let me ask you this. Say you're from Texas. That means you likely have family and a few friends there still, right? They could be your eyes and ears (your "bird dogs"). Or you could rely on the Internet for your initial due diligence. Have you ever tried the Google Satellite experience? If not, I invite you to go to www.GoogleMaps.com and hit the satellite view option. Enter the street address of your home and keep clicking the plus sign. Click on the little person icon and drag it where you want to "stand." You can be "standing" in front of your home. You can take a "stroll" up and down the street to look at the neighborhood. It's a little unnerving and most of the time the images are a bit outdated. However, the point of this experiment is to show you that you can look at property anywhere with this method, so you can see what the area looks like, if it is really run down, if it's nice, if it's groomed, if it's dangerous-looking, etc. You can see the types of vehicles parked in front of the homes, whether there are broken windows, bars on the windows, nice flower gardens and more. Broken windows are not necessarily a bad thing. That might be a problem to fix. A solution you can provide. Remember that you are the provider of solutions. You find and

fix problems. You will be valued for being that person… THAT investor.

Let's take a few steps to the right on the map of the U.S. to another state and another city. Let's look at Detroit. At the time of this writing, Detroit is in big trouble financially. The city declared bankruptcy! This could be your time to shine, to be the hero, to help people through real estate investing. Notice I didn't say your time to make big money off of other people's pain and suffering. You cannot ever take that attitude. Well, I can't anyway. I won't. If my real estate investing efforts can't do some good, I am not interested. Again, and you'll hear this throughout the book, I want to provide people with a place to live, work, lay and play. I am going to look at real estate with a bigger picture and goal in mind than just what money I can make from the deal. If you take this same attitude, your bank account will grow exponentially along with your ability to do good and leave a legacy. I would rather be known as the problem solver who came in and provided clean, safe, affordable housing to a lot of families and a place to live and play in other countries than a real estate investor who made tons of money.

Now back to Detroit…

It is a given that some politician will earmark a lot of money in government aide for the bankrupted Detroit, so necessary improvements can be made to create a good space for people to live, work, play and lay again. That is an opportunity for real estate investors. Think BIG here. What if YOU could be the person to provide much-needed fire stations, schools, police stations and the like? What if you could provide these things to facilitate privatization of these facets of the community to help reduce the cost of having those fundamental needs of the people met in the areas of protection and education? And what about housing? Detroit has a terrific historical significance to our country. If I say the word "Detroit" what do you immediately think of? That's right. It was the hub of commerce and industry in the last century, and it brought manufacturing to the forefront across a variety of industries. The city also has gorgeous – or what could be gorgeous – historical residential areas. In fact, many of these areas are listed in the National Register of Historic Places.

What does all this mean to you as a real estate investor? Maybe you love the idea of historical preservation and building museums or creating museums from some of the historical homes in Detroit. Maybe you could get other investors on board with your vision to rebuild parts of the historic districts in Detroit. Maybe you create new fire stations and police stations or a hospital. Or maybe you invest other people's money (and they give it to you because you made them see your vision) in an old apartment building. Then you renovate it to provide good, safe, affordable housing for families. In the process you create cash flow for yourself, too.

Renovating not your cup of tea? What about uncommon investment opportunities? Perhaps investing in timeshares would interest you. Stay with me here. A new timeshare property can sell for hundreds of thousands of dollars over

time. However, what if the timeshare owner falls behind in taxes, association dues and maintenance fees? That's an opportunity for a real estate investor. There are businesses created around this concept. They buy and sell gently used timeshares. All timeshares are gently used, because their owners don't really get to use them much. Most are lucky to spend two weeks a year in their timeshare. However, the model is appealing to many people. If they appeal to you, maybe you should look into timeshare properties in Detroit. You agree to pick up the back taxes and other dues, and you negotiate a far-below-market rate in the price. You hold onto the timeshare until such time as an opportunity, such as a major sports event or championship, appears. Bingo! You have a rental property. I'm not saying that Detroit will be chosen for the next Olympics, but there will be opportunities in the future and you need to keep your eyes and ears open if you are thinking about investing in rebuilding Detroit. If it becomes a great historical resort destination, get there now and invest. Wait. (Buy and hold.) When Detroit becomes a place where people want to stay and play, you'll see continued returns on your investment.

That's what the international investing I'm doing is all about for my family and me. (Oh, didn't I tell you? I am investing internationally!) It is absolutely thrilling to be a part of this deal. We are building in an area where people will be coming to play. We will own a significant portion (at least significant to us) of the amenities and surrounding fun activities to augment the experience. To add entertainment. (Remember that everything, including entertainment, is real estate.) The project is also going to be a sustainable community, complete with restaurants and other activities to keep residents and guests entertained. A portion of our net profits each and every month will go directly to charitable groups, too. I can't tell you how excited I am about that! It is all a part of my long-term vision that I set into motion a couple of years back.

Have vision to the distant future.

Talking about long-term vision, let's take a trip (on Google) to South Dakota and Mt. Rushmore. Someone had a vision for that area. People invested in land there, because one day it would make a great destination. These people, these everyday visionaries, were correct. And now Mt. Rushmore, a piece of real estate, offers a place to stay and play for an astounding three million people annually. Want to learn more about this type of investing? Hold on. You'll learn more about this type of "out of the box" thinking in Step Eight.

Now, back to Detroit again. (Is your head spinning yet with all this travel?) Maybe you should consider buying and holding land in that area. If you have a vision for what the area could be with the right investments in its real estate market, wouldn't it be a wise choice? I am not advising you to run out and buy up all the land in Detroit. I'm asking you to SEE the possibilities, to weigh out the options and do your research. That last step is critical. You cannot invest in any real estate without all the facts. Doing your "due diligence" will help to keep you from losing money. I'm getting to the process soon.

Keep reading.

Don't miss opportunities!

You know one way that assures your losing money? It is by passing over good opportunities. If you don't think this is true, I'll let you in on my missed opportunity. I had a chance to invest in a deal that I didn't fully understand. Instead of taking the mindset that I'd do my homework and I'd let others handle all the parts I don't understand and moving ahead, I said, "No, thanks. I'll pass." [Hitting myself on the forehead with the palm of my hand here.] The other investor got money from someone else and moved ahead without me. He went on to earn $1M in profit. Half of that amount would have been mine had I not passed the deal up. Why did I NOT do it? Because I wanted to figure out everything for myself before taking action. The opportunity passed; I can't get it back.

Here's another form of missed opportunities. It comes from a guy who shouted out a problem in one of my workshops. Actually, he asked a question, but his problem to be solved was shouting at me. The man tells me that he is putting out bandit signs, dropping business cards, doing this and doing that. Then he said, "I get confused about what I'm looking for. Sometimes I am looking for people who want to contribute capital; sometimes I am looking for people who have a property or who just want to learn more. What do I need to say to get them interested in what I am doing?"

My response? "There is the problem. You are only focused on what you need to say, what you want and what you're looking for. The problem is that you are not asking any questions about what it is that THEY need. That is the secret."

Case in point, with one person that I was able to get hundreds of thousands of dollars from (i.e., greater than half a million dollars), the conversation started because he said; "I have a tax problem."

I said, "Cool. I can help you with that. How big is your tax problem?"

He told me the scope of the problem and I said, "Cool. Well, in order to solve that tax problem, this is what we need to do. We need to buy a really big piece of real estate and then… boom, boom, boom… Then we check with your accountant and if he confirms what I just said then we should get this done." He agreed and the result of that deal is one of the buildings that I am rehabbing today. This didn't happen because I asked him, "Do you have hundreds of thousands of dollars you can give me so I can pay you a 5%, 9%, 12% return?" That was not even part of the conversation. The deal happened because I was listening for his problem. That's why I ask so many questions (even if they annoy people). I need to know the problem. If I don't know the problem, then I don't know how to respond. I will give you more examples later. I shared this with you now, because if I hadn't asked a lot of questions of this man to learn his problem, I wouldn't have purchased an apartment building, which would have been a huge missed opportunity!

Regarding missed opportunities by over-thinking things, let's say you have an opportunity to go to the movies with friends. Your goal is to go to the store first to get a few things that you need first and then you can meet with your friends. But then you decide you can't get into the car until you've mapped out your trip completely, buffed out the car and you've done a number of other tasks. You end up never going out. You missed your opportunity to have fun with your friends by over-thinking the process. You think true visionaries in real estate over-think things? They don't. They see an opportunity and they take it. They take the risks, too.

Let me direct your attention to one such visionary. This one lived in what is now Irvine, Calif., about 200 years ago. Born in 1827 in Ireland, Mr. James Irvine became the co-founder of the Irvine Ranch. Hold up! It wasn't that simple. First he had to take a series of action steps. First there was the potato famine that pushed his brother and him to the United States. Second, he landed and worked in New York. Then, in 1848, he joined the California Gold Rush as a merchant and miner. He must have done okay, because in 1854 he purchased an interest in a company in San Francisco that would be renamed Irvine Company. James continued investing in real estate and businesses, amassing great wealth. Along the way, he married twice and created children who continued forward with what their father taught them in real estate investing. They made their way to southern California, where they bought up about a third of the land in present-day Orange County. The city of Irvine was named after James' son (James Irvine, II) and the rest is history. Irvine Company continues to reign supreme in Orange County. It is a very strong company, thanks to the foresight and investment practices of the first James Irvine who saw opportunity everywhere. Perhaps Detroit can be the next Irvine if only the right real estate investors were to see the possibilities. Is that person you?

Avoiding money loss starts with homework.

There are lots of ways to lose money in real estate, but educating yourself prior to making investment decisions isn't one of them. If you don't want to lose money in the market, be smart about what you do. When I say make more deals faster, I'm not telling you to close your eyes and make blind decisions. Quite the contrary. DO YOUR HOMEWORK. Research the properties. Think about what the area could be one day. Don't overlook land deals either. Maybe that big slice of land you've found would be ideal one day for a university setting. You don't have to build the university, but you can sell your land to the guy who wants to, right? Or you could lease the land. That's something to explore, too. (And it would be a smart move.)

As an experiment, find some properties in an area other than where you live (unless you happen to live in Texas, Detroit or another big-opportunity area) and browse. Gather details about the area. You could start your search on an aggregation site, like www.Bid4Assets.com or www.EconoHomes.com, where properties are gathered (aggregated for you already by region and type). These sites are designed much like a Costco

and they can be beneficial to your efforts as a wholesaler or when you are looking for profitable rental property. Why do I say "like Costco"? In Costco, you can buy a big box of soda, take the cans out of the package and drop them in an ice chest to resell (with the right permits, of course). In this example, a 24-can box of soda may cost you $3.99. Of course, we have to add in for state recycling taxes, so maybe that price gets bumped up to $5 or $6. Repackaged, each cold can of refreshment brings a minimum of $1 per unit. That's $18 or more in profit. You are repackaging something good and making it better for a profit. The same can be said with the real estate-aggregation sites. They are offering discount real estate to investors who can then turn around and sell them at a profit, but not until they have been adequately repackaged. For example, fixing what is broken or adding things that will improve the renter's or new owner's life. It takes research to find the good product, however. And that takes good interpersonal and communication skills. Yes, that is a recurrent theme of this book.

Okay. Don't make a bid just yet. You aren't done. It's not that easy. Sorry. It's not and it never will be. For now, just pick a couple of properties and then it's time to do your research. On these sites, they do some of the legwork for you, but you cannot count on everything you read to be accurate or up to date. Humans run these sites, which means mistakes can and do happen. You should call the county where the property is located and ask questions. You need to know if there are issues or "encumbrances" on the property. (Back taxes or other pesky issues.) For the sake of argument, let's say you find a property and it is good. Or at least it looks good. What is your next step? Google the address. Take a tour of the area virtually. What do you see? What can you learn? Call the county and get as much information on the property as you possibly can. (You see why knowing someone in the area would be helpful?)

NOTE: Keep your findings for the next step. We are going further with this research and how to be thorough before making an investment decision. Be clear in your goals, too.

Are your goals clearly defined?

People ask me what I think about their goals. They tell me that so-and-so in their life has told them that the goal is too big or very unrealistic. They express their feelings of insecurity that they have about their goal, because they are buying into the negative-speak of those people in their inner circle of friends and family. Here's what I say to anyone who asks me what I think about the goal. First, why do they care what I think? Second, there is no such thing as an unrealistic goal! There are unrealistic time frames, however, and that's where real estate investors need to be mindful. Setting a big time frame, like 20 years to achieve a big goal, is more accurate than setting an unrealistic goal of, say, building a resort in two years. Get real with yourself. Set a goal and if it's pretty big, tell people that it may take 20 years to achieve. You can achieve it. That's the truth. Likely you'll achieve your goal in far less than 20 years if it's something you truly want and can see in your mind's eye clearly.

124

My first goal was to earn $10K per month. To me at that time, just six years ago, that was a big goal. It didn't take as long as I had thought it would take to reach my goal and then surpass it. There's a reason. We as human beings underestimate what we can accomplish in a year's time or just a handful of years. Once your goal is clear, you are also cleared for takeoff. As T. Harv Eker would say, "Clarity leads to power." We all have the power to decide and to act. Go for it, and don't let anyone stop you. When this happened for my wife and me, we took off. We didn't stop and we didn't look back. We certainly didn't slow down. Now when I look at what my team and I accomplish in one week's time it sometimes blows my mind! I am grateful beyond words for my team's assistance and belief in our goals. To think… all it took was a lot of hard work, developing a new skill set of interpersonal and communication skills, and gathering leads and resources! Actually, that last one is easy once you've developed your interpersonal skills. Oh, and another thing is that you need to stop listening to lies. We'll get to that in the next step!

NOTE: Right before we took this book to print, I opened a new website designed to help you get into real estate investing by providing rental-ready properties great for the buy-and-hold investor. If you are a wholesaler, you need to check the site out; if you are a buy-and-hold type, you need to check it out; if you work with investors looking for single-family homes, you need to check it out. The site is www.BeginInvestingNow. com and like everything else we do in our team, we are moving quickly to expand our offerings and the types of properties. I hope you will visit and give me your input!

STEP FOUR

Stop Listening to Lies

"Think twice before you speak, because your words and influence will plant the seed of either success or failure in the mind of another." Napoleon Hill

This step might not be what you'd expect. You might think I'm going to tell you that you need to stop listening to all the nay-sayers who tell you that you can't be a real estate investor, that because you don't have money and your credit score is below 600 that you have no chance at buying real estate, and that you're silly to think you'll succeed at this game. Okay, that's all true. You can make it; don't listen to the nay-sayers; you can buy property with zero money in your bank account and with terrible credit. Further, though we call it the real estate "game," investing in real estate is not a game. It is a whole lot of fun, however, and it's something people like me... just like YOU... do every day, every week and every year to keep good sums of cash flowing through their bank accounts.

Understanding this last point, do you know what you don't really need when you have cash flow? A great credit score! It doesn't hurt you to have one, but you certainly don't need one. I'm living proof. You think my credit score was high when I made my first investment deal? Uh, no... (Go back and read Step One.)

If those were the only lies around real estate investing, this would be a short section. Obviously, that's not the case and I'm nowhere near done. Here are things you will hear in this industry that simply are NOT true:

"It's easy!"
"Everyone will succeed."
"Everyone can do it."

If you have heard these things and buy into them, I am here to burst your bubble.

Real estate investing is not "easy." There is a lot of hard work and effort involved on the part of several people (your team and additional professionals). You will work hard to achieve your success as a real estate problem solver!

Everyone will not succeed. Many will enter the race, but not every horse will be a winner. Fewer still will stick it out. Quite a number of those who decide to participate in real estate will have a failure event and give up. They won't try again. The truth is that everyone CAN succeed, but many will walk away before succeeding. Not everyone actually can do it.

128

Real estate investing is not for everyone. Those who cannot handle making mistakes and can't pick themselves up and dust themselves off to try and try again likely aren't great candidates for this line of work. It is work, you know? For me it's a perfect fit! My top skills happen to be interpersonal communications, public speaking and sales. In the world of real estate investing, that's a golden skill set! It's also a set of skills I developed over time. None of it just came naturally. I realized these skills were absolutely necessary and I honed them. I love what I do in my life. I love using real estate investing to make positive change in other people's lives. I couldn't imagine doing anything different.

I spend more time talking to people about my mistakes than my successes. But then every success comes from a series of mistakes. Look at the Colonel Sanders story. That man made a huge mistake. He didn't consult with the planning committee in his city before building his first chicken stand. He didn't do his homework or research. If he had we might never have gotten to experience KFC chicken, and that would be a shame. Because Col. Sanders didn't know the city planned to build a freeway where he had built his first chicken stand, he was forced to move and then to move on to develop a new plan. KFC was the result. That didn't happen overnight. The colonel made more mistakes and more mistakes, and then he learned from them and got his plan into action the right way. (Right now, you might be seeing the colonel in his white top coat on the bucket of your favorite KFC chicken. I know I am.)

There is no such thing as "overnight success." I'm sure you've seen ads that tell you that you can "do it overnight" when talking about making it big in real estate. Or maybe you've been enticed to sign up for an event because you can learn everything you need to know in a "three-day boot camp" and all you have to do is "follow these simple steps and you won't make a mistake." Okay. Sure. If you believe that hype, it's time for me to get real with you. Nothing happens overnight! (It took me a good four months to close my first deal. You see, there was a learning curve. Everyone has a learning curve. I just happen to apply instruction quickly.) You don't learn everything you need to know to do anything right once you leave the seminar. And even if you follow every step of all programs as the experts lay out for you that doesn't mean instant success. Remember, first comes the knowledge, then the application of that knowledge, then mistakes because you are human and humans make mistakes. Then and only then can you achieve success.

Remember this: You cannot learn something new AND look good doing it. Learning how to walk is one of those things, right? What if my two-year-old said, "Dad, I'm not gonna learn to walk till I look good doing it"? Same goes for your learning how to maneuver your way in real estate. It's okay to stumble, fall and fail. These are required to become successful. Did you know that a lot of our inventions and innovations are a result of great mistakes? Yes! Read *Mistakes That Work* by Charlotte Jones. It's a good read with excellent information.

What is information anyway?

Information is only relevant to the time line. Let's say you heard someone in real estate speak at an event in 1998. He was right on target with his information in the 90s, but now his information wouldn't necessarily be correct or applicable to our current economic and housing market situation. Some of it might. I won't discount that. However, techniques that worked well two decades ago likely won't today. But sometimes we are so desperate for A SOLUTION that we accept any solution. We accept outdated information. Don't do that. Educate yourself so you know if what you are learning about investing in real estate is relevant to today's conditions.

I laugh when I hear some investors say that "before the housing market got so bad" they were doing great. As they reminisce about the "good ol' days" I shake my head. All I've known is a down market. I did okay. I did more than okay. You will never hear me say that what I've done and what I continue to do is easy. It is not. I'm still learning new things. I continue to educate myself about tax laws, real estate laws in different states, negotiation practices and anything else I can get my hands on that will help me in the next deal and the next and the next. If you visit my website at www. CashFlowDiary.com, you will see that I share with you the books I read. Why do I do that? Because they are excellent books with great information that any real estate investor or entrepreneur can put to use immediately. Read them. They will help you on your path to success.

You can't put success in the microwave!

That's the truth. People want instant success, but it doesn't work that way. You can't stick success in the microwave and hit a few buttons and achieve it in 45 seconds. To attain success in anything you do in life takes time and hard work. If it didn't, everyone would do what I do. Everyone would do what you do. Where's the fun in that? (If everyone is special no one is special. You ever hear that one?)

You want to be successful in real estate? Talk less and listen more! Stop arguing that "your way" works better when you have zero proof of that statement. Often, people approach me at events to tell me they are interested in getting into real estate and say, "I heard you are supposed to do it [this way]!" Then they go on to explain what they have learned or their beliefs in how things should go in real estate investing. I'm a fairly patient man. I listen. Then I ask them what results they've generated with this technique that they've just spent so much time explaining to me. Bupkis! No results at all. That's the difference between theory and buying into lies vs. real-world understanding and practice. If your "technique" has brought you zero results and the way I'm sharing with you here in how to do real estate deals has brought me 380+ units and counting, which formula should you use? I'm just asking.

Some might call my approach confrontational. I call it CAREFRONTATIONAL. I care about your outcome in real estate investing. I mean what I say. I practice each and every

day exactly what I teach. I don't talk theory. I talk about what actually will work for you. In my moments of Carefrontation™ I promise that I will risk offending you – even publicly if I have to, so you will listen – to help you get what you want.

I'm going to steer you away from listening to lies about real estate investing. Not just those we've covered, but a few more that have to do with us as a society and what we are told to believe. One is retirement. Another lie is something we discussed a bit before about getting a job so we can earn a paycheck.

The myth about retirement.

In episode #5 of my Cash Flow Diary podcast, I go into depth about why retirement plans may sound great but really aren't. I invite you to log in and listen from my website. It would be a great complement to what you are reading here. I'll give you the short version right now, but you have to promise to check out the podcast and give me your feedback and questions. Okay? Okay.

We are taught that saving our hard-earned dollars for retirement is a smart thing. Heck, when I was helping clients as a financial planner, I did my part to expand that message, but it is incorrect thinking. At least for today's economic climate where interest rates on savings are abysmally low. It's good for me as an investor though, because I can offer an investor more than the 3.5% interest they would be lucky to get in their traditional retirement plan to participate in one of my deals.

In the fiction that dictates that we must save a big pile of cash so we can earn money over time on that pile of green to be able to retire nicely, you have to save a bundle. A financial planner will likely tell you that to save the amount of money you need – if you live in southern California that number needs to be into the millions of dollars – you need to save at minimum $500 a month and maybe as much as $2,500 a month. You put that into your don't-touch-it-till-you-retire account. Upon retirement you get to start "living" on that money plus the "whopping" amount of interest you earned over time. This myth about saving for retirement is actually what drives people over the age of 65 to go back to work. Do they want to? No. But they find out that even though they saved their money, there were a lot of variables that they and apparently their "well-educated" financial planner didn't take into consideration. For example, taxes and inflation. Hello!

A financial planner might tell you that you need to decide how much it would take RIGHT NOW for you to live comfortably. For the sake of discussion, let's say the number is $10,000 a month. Excellent. That also means that when you are no longer working and you have $10,000 a month coming in steadily you then get to call yourself retired. Now comes the fun part. You put your money in the bank in a retirement account that earns (for the sake of discussion) 3.49%. You pay zero taxes on the money while you are saving it. That sounds good. Now let's say you want to live for 20 years on your retirement. Doing

quick calculations that are based on your proposed $10,000 a month, that means you have to save $3.4M for retirement. Can you do that? Most people can't. It's not even logical. Not to mention, the costs of living now vs. what the costs of living will be in a decade or more will be vastly different. To cement this idea in your mind, think about gas prices that dictate many of the other costs of living. How much was a gallon of gas two decades ago? How much now? Exactly!

The better solution is to be "retired" now by building your real estate portfolio with pieces that produce income for you every month. Or take real estate out of the scenario and produce a product or service that you can sell to create the $10,000 a month you say you need to live comfortably. Produce streams of income that you control. Not the bank. Not some ridiculously low interest rate.

Believing the retirement savings myth starts in kindergarten.

The reason we are lead to believe that all we have to do is save big for retirement and we'll be able to have a comfy life in our later years is because we are spoon fed this idea between kindergarten and the twelfth grade. We aren't taught financial intelligence. We aren't taught emotional intelligence. We are taught to believe what we are told and to not ask questions. We are told to work hard in school, gain academic intelligence and then graduate to get a job so we can what? That's right. So we can learn how to do that job. One would think that if we put in all that time in school we might already know how to do the job upon graduation. After all, didn't we get "the job" because we earned good marks in that area of study? That brings into question so many jobs that our college graduates accept. If you go into a profession such as becoming a medical doctor, psychotherapist, CPA or attorney, I can see the point of putting in all that time in school. However, there are a lot of professions that make me scratch my head when I learn of how much school the individual went through to start at the absolute bottom rung of a business only to have to claw their way up the ladder.

I also know people who didn't earn a college degree who entered a business and worked their way up the ladder the same way. Guess what? Some of them made it all the way to the top to be VPs of big departments in banks and other large corporations. I also know of people who earned top degrees in college and were eventually laid off from very high-paying jobs only to end up serving lines of customers in a food court. What I'm saying here is that wouldn't it be better if we were to teach kids in school actual financial and emotional intelligence and give them the tools to go out into the world and earn an income not based on a degree but rather based on their abilities to create streams of income? Wouldn't it be great if we stopped telling kids they have to work really hard in school and then get out to find a J-O-B? Talk to my oldest daughter. She'll set you straight. She attends high school and she gets good grades, but she knows the realities of life and how sands can shift without warning. She watched her mother and I struggle, and she watched us overcome our troubles by being entrepreneurially minded. She must have been taking notes, because her business is doing well. She even uses the crocheted items she creates to sell to make money for herself to fund school sports programs. If she can embrace the concept of self-education and implementing entrepreneurial skills, what about you? That's my challenge to you.

What's one final really big lie in real estate?

"You have to start in real estate in your own back yard. You have to start with your own money and your own credit." Wait… WHAT? No. If that's the case, explain it to me. Explain what my team and I have accomplished in a few short years. I don't know if I could have done so well had I only invested in my own back yard. We have some pretty expensive back yards here in Orange County!

Remember our discussion in the last section about buying and selling properties in Memphis? While some of my very first deals were in my own back yard, I quickly moved into another market. I didn't over-think it; I just did it. I jumped into the pool and started swimming. I made deals. At one point I got into fix 'n' flip, but that didn't work out for me. However, that experience was invaluable. The huge mistakes I made were a gift. I learned more in that one raw deal than I could ever have in years of book learning. Doing is what got me here. Doing is what will get you to your goals.

Think of me at this moment as your personal real estate fitness trainer. Imagine that I'm walking with you to look at a property that you have researched and have found to be an excellent investment. What am I saying to you? JUST DO IT! Make an offer. Then do it again. Take the first step, then the next and the next. You'll get good at this. There is no substitution for execution. The education system doesn't provide the necessary information and won't give you the wisdom you need to do well as a real estate investor. The secret is to just keep doing and then do some more.

Think you can't do deals? I challenge you!

In my one-on-one calls and my Mastermind Group sessions, I talk about four different ways to buy real estate, which are lease options, contract for deed, "Subject To" and purchase money mortgage. But none of this matters if you aren't willing to take a chance and get out there. None of it matters if you aren't willing to make offers. I want you to do it. I'm going to keep pushing you to make offers and to implement what you learn immediately. Don't wait.

Moving at the speed of instruction makes your life different. Unquestioning action makes a difference. Just keep it simple. When I teach people about real estate investing I look for the right mindset. For example, if I'm teaching a seminar, I look for the people who really want to take action. If the right person has a right mindset he/she will say, "Show me what I need to do and I'll do it at the next break." Then they take immediate action. They don't wait till they get home and deal with the kids or their job or whatever.

Here's the deal… "If it's going to make you money," I tell people, "then get up from the event and go make that call!" Some do, but many don't. That's sad. Sometimes I get a person who will challenge me big time. Challenge is good! At one seminar I was challenged to make a call about a property in front of the group. So I did. I had to practice what I was teaching, right? This is how I got one of my apartment buildings! No kidding.

Why do I challenge people to make offers? Sure, I care, but beyond that I want everyone to know that if they get over their fears of making phone calls and if they do it right away that they will have success.

At one seminar where I was teaching negotiation skills, I was looking for properties as examples online in front of the class. I found a really good one. A guy in the audience said I couldn't do it… I couldn't get the property. Okay. I like a good challenge. So I called on the property over the speaker on my phone, so the whole class could hear and benefit from the negotiation. The property was bank-owned and listed at a price. It was the suggested price. I offered a far lower price. The property was worth a lot more than what I offered. Remember, an offer is only an invitation for conversation! (I tell people to write the offer for one dollar and if the seller says yes… great! Hey, why not? At least it opens conversation.)

In the example, the list price is just a suggestion. It was a 70-unit apartment building. I offered $500 per unit. The class went stone cold quiet. I heard crickets! I had no intention at

that moment of buying the building and I didn't have the cash, but I ended up with an invitation to talk. When the people I called came back to me, they said no to my original offer but countered with, "How about $100,000?" I came back with, "How about $60,000?" They said YES. I turned to the class and said, "Who's in?" I didn't get any takers from the class, which is fine. It was a lesson from which they could all learn. I was able to find investors from my contacts list.

If you are new to real estate investing you might be facing certain challenges, not just in your thinking but also with the thinking of other people in your life. You might be asking yourself, "How do I do what J. tells me to do when everyone around me is telling me I shouldn't try?" That one can be tough for some, but you aren't "some." You decided to be an action-step person, someone who doesn't just try. You are someone who tries and tries again and then DOES what he/she sets out to do. If you don't already know what I'm about to tell you, I'm not sure where your mind has been so far in this book. To succeed, you have to stop listening to lies. That includes listening to the negativity of others, even of those you love. Their negativity can impact you and stop you in your tracks. Reject the negativity of others. Stop doubting yourself. Change your mindset! That will require a little brain training, and that's what we cover next. Getting to your goals is all about the process of manifestation. Stay tuned.

STEP FIVE

Train Your Brain: Mindset Matters!

"Do you want to know who you are? Don't ask. Act! Action will delineate and define you." Thomas Jefferson

You want to be a real estate investor? You will have to change your mindset. This is a critical step. How you think about the world and about your abilities matters… a lot. You have to put yourself in the position to receive changes in your life. It's not just a matter of asking to receive; you have to believe the things you want are actually possible. If you see people when you are out and about, and they look happy and fulfilled, do you find yourself wondering how in the heck they achieved the life they have? Here's the secret. They allowed themselves the life they saw in their minds. They then took the necessary action steps that put them in that picture. Simply, they adjusted their mindset. It's like turning the dial from "off" to "on" or opening a door. Do it and then step through it! This takes initiative and then you have to go through a process of manifestation to go from having an idea to bringing that idea into being.

Take initiative in your life.

I contributed to a book written by Greg S. Reid entitled Initiative in which the writer cleverly leads readers through the process of how we can change our mindset over time to adapt to new possibilities. However, first we must believe before we can achieve. In the book, I came in at chapter 7, where creative commercial financing is discussed. In this chapter, I show the main character Morgan – a 40-something woman who is laid off from a lackluster, unfulfilling job – that she can have her dream of business ownership. I make it possible in a way that she never dreamed. I won't be a spoiler in case you want to read the book, but in short I help Morgan attain entrepreneurship, which brings happiness and fulfillment to her life, through a little creative financing to help her get into a retail space quickly. However, before this step, Morgan had to be open to the idea that her dream business could really be hers. To get to this point, she had to change the way she viewed herself and her life. She had to understand that money or the lack thereof is not what was holding her back or keeping her in a boring, unsatisfying job and life.

In the book, Morgan takes a series of small action steps. Some are larger than others. She takes initiative toward what she wants in life. And you know what they say… a body in motion tends to stay in motion! But no motion would occur until

Morgan embraced the truth that she could have the life she saw others having, others who really were happy and fulfilled in all they do. This makes all the sense in the world, because Morgan (just like the rest of us) is on a spiritual journey. There is a spiritual aspect to us as humans. What we tie ourselves to in our minds is what we tie ourselves to in reality. Why tie yourself down when you can fly?

If you are reading these words and they hit home, if you are not satisfied, not happy and do not feel fulfilled in different areas of your life, I invite you to take the same journey of the mind that Morgan does in Initiative. Start visualizing what you really want and understand that it is yours if you will take the action steps necessary to achieve it. Further, you must practice every day to change your mindset. How? All I can do is tell you what I did and have you follow that model. I started with a Vision Book. You learned about that in the opening of this book, so I won't repeat myself here. However, this Vision Book was part of my "process of manifestation" and it was an excellent tool to help me carry my ideas into reality.

These are pages from my very first Vision Book!

The process of manifestation explained…

How do things come into being? How does anything move from an idea to something tangible or something we use every day? It is through the process of manifestation. It is not a complicated process. Here is how I explain it in episode #4 of my Cash Flow Diary podcast:

All things begin with an idea. If you have a thought for long enough it begins to create certain feelings. Those feelings persist long enough until they become beliefs. Those beliefs grow stronger and at some point motivate you to take action. Then you create activity. As you go out into the world to create activity, you begin to develop and experience results. You get enough of those results and what begin to form are habits. Develop enough of these habits or repeat those habits consistently over time, and they begin to shape your character. From your character, you reap your destiny.

The process is a progression of thought and activity. In this, your character plays a mighty role. When I say "character" I really mean all of the things for which you are absolutely known. For example, maybe you're known for speeding. I have a heavy foot when I'm driving so maybe I'm projecting onto you a little bit, but let's just say that like me you enjoy driving fast. That is something you are known to do. It is a part of your character. This speeding character trait can translate into other areas of your life. For example, let's look at me again. I am known for not always looking carefully before I leap or jumping ahead in a lot of ways. That's just part of who I am. In fact, I often tell people that I'm the guy who is more like "fire, aim, ready?" That's how I describe myself. I'm more that type of person vs. the more careful and planned "ready, aim, fire!" type. There is nothing wrong with the way I am. In fact, it serves me well. Besides, I have a number of "ready, aim, fire" types by my side who can keep me in check.

Maybe you are more a "ready, ready, ready, aim, ready, aim, aim, ready…" type. If so, you need to adjust your character. That way of thinking won't get you very far, because you completely change subjects and never fire. It's time to move into being a more action-taking type of person. You will be better served if you change your beliefs about yourself and your abilities. You can do way more than you think. This is something I guarantee, but how will you know if you never take true aim and fire?

So, let's recap. A thought leads to a feeling that leads to a belief. Then it is activity that leads to results that instill good habits that help to build your character. With this chain in place you are brought to your destiny. Rather, you create your destiny. What's my point? You have to start in order to get anywhere. I practice what I'm teaching you. Go browse my site. Did everything you see there just come to be overnight? No. It all started with a single thought. I wanted to share my knowledge with individuals like you who were interested enough in creating cash flow through real estate. Okay… honestly, I wasn't that smart. I actually am concerned about ensuring that I leave one of my most important assets to my children, which is what I've learned and experienced. Then the idea came to me that if I was going to make a diary of sorts with all the great stuff that I learned to help in a way that my kids would be able to get it, I bet there'd be at least one adult that would be interested, as well. So I took steps. Now I'm writing this book. That also began as a thought. Okay, other people told me I needed to do it, but those people's comments and suggestions planted the idea that took root and grew.

I don't care about whatever your idea happens to be…
whether it is to own a business or you want to build, maintain
and grow a portfolio of real estate that will help you live
better now and into retirement, I want you to water that idea.
Take action and the activity will help to build your character
and abilities. Before you know it you will be looking back,
wondering why you didn't take action sooner on your idea(s).
This process of manifestation works for everything across the
board in life. You think I always believed this? Not really. But
I need to give you a bit more of a look into my upbringing.
Then you'll understand where I'm coming from. (And literally
where I came from!)

Upbringing has its affects.

Again, environment holds a lot of weight in our lives.
Environment is powerful. Sometimes we have to overcome
our environment to become successful at a chosen profession,
especially when it goes against other people's ideals of what
our lives should be. How would I know that? I come from a
military family. A lot of my family grew up in an area of North
Carolina known as Savoy Heights. Go to Savoy Heights today
and, yes, you will find drug dealers on many corners, etc. It is
not all that great of an area. My family also lived on Murchison
Road in North Carolina, which wasn't much better. I primarily
grew up overseas, but for the first four years of my life I was
raised in Alaska with my mom's older sister and her husband.
I now realize the very profound effect these years with my
aunt and uncle had on me, like when it comes to academics.

It was something that they stressed highly. I was able to read and do math well before I entered kindergarten. That's when I reunited with my mom, who eventually married a guy in the military who happened to play basketball and fix cars. My stepfather was stereotypically manly and stressed "manly" things, which just wasn't me. I was more into computers. Yes, I was a geek. I admit it.

At the age of seven I got my first computer, and it changed my world. It was a Commodore VIC-20 and I excelled at dissecting computer code in steps to make the computer do something. That was what I considered fun. (It was also something that would end up serving me well later in life.) Instead of going outside to play, what I wanted to do was play with the computer. It was awesome! I rewrote a lot of code back then. I'd get magazines that had sample coding. I could copy the code and make things work. I could do it, which made me feel great. It was a long time ago. By then I was in Germany where I spent 11 years of my life. If you need to know the dates, that's 1979 through 1990.

I got a lot out of my experience overseas. First, I wasn't in the environment of Savoy Heights and all the stuff that came with it. I was exposed to a lot of positive things that I wouldn't otherwise be exposed to, like museums, a different culture and other people's languages. If you are in the military or you have a military upbringing you know what I'm saying here. Because we were stationed in West Germany before the wall came down, we were able to visit Czechoslovakia and Prague. We visited Italy back when they had the Lira and I learned

about exchange rates. I got to visit Anne Frank's house as a field trip. We read the book, *The Diary of Anne Frank*, and then said, "Hey, let's go there!" Okay, why not?

Though I saw amazing things and had incredible opportunities, I was a kid. No matter what, no matter where, kids get in trouble. Peer pressure can send us down a wrong path. I took that path for a short time. I had to learn to say no to people for things like shoplifting and whatnot, because I realized my bad behaviors and poor choices hurt my mother. I had to learn that lesson, but her feelings weren't the only reason for me to straighten out. If you're a child in a military family and if you do something stupid, especially overseas, it actually affects your dad and his job. That's bad news.

For whatever reason I didn't learn that lesson fast enough. That was not good. (This is how I got introduced to the police.) After that I learned that just because you're in a foreign country doesn't mean rules don't apply to you. If you like to push and bend rules, you find out pretty quickly that you can get in trouble. If you are lucky in youth like I was, you also get to learn about second chances. That's good. I would find out that I'd need a few second chances in my life. (I never stopped looking at "rules" differently, however, which ended up being a very good thing.)

My stepdad was very strict; it was an occupational hazard. He was the consummate military man. To give you an example, in my house on Christmas morning we did things a little differently than other kids. It wasn't about rushing to the tree

149

and ripping open presents. No. We had something else. Our Christmas morning entailed making sure that we cleaned our rooms and made our beds military-style before we got to open presents. (You could bounce a dime off my bed!) It wasn't horrible. It was just a different experience. It was an idiosyncrasy on the part of my stepfather.

There are many little idiosyncrasies that Army brats like me might recognize if I were to share more stories here. For example, Army brats might understand why I feel the strong urge to stand at attention before a movie starts. Growing up on a military base meant that when we went to the movie theatre we would stand up and salute the flag while the National Anthem played in the background. When we were done the movie would start. If you're an Army brat, you might also understand that at 5 o'clock in the morning and 5 o'clock in the evening, no matter what you're doing, you might stop in your tracks. You're waiting to hear *Reveille* in the morning and *Retreat* in the evening. On base the sound is like a foghorn, loud and clear, so everyone hears it. Cars literally pull off to the side of the road and stop. Then people get out and stand at attention, facing whatever flag they can find, and they wait. It is a different experience, and I'm thankful for it.

Want to hear something strange? As I grew up I didn't see a penny, like a literal penny, until I came back to the U.S. Why? They didn't have pennies in Germany! I didn't grow up with commercials either, because they didn't have commercials in Germany. They had public service announcements. TV on its regular schedule was a season or two behind the U.S.,

so communication with the people stateside was always odd when they talked about TV. People back home would regularly send us TV shows that were recorded so we could keep current. That was in the days of Betamax! Believe me, I learned to enjoy recorded Saturday morning cartoons.

I love sharing these stories with my kids. They look at me like I'm from another planet. It's like I'm telling them ghost stories. No? Really, Dad? Yes, really. And I trudged uphill in the snow… both ways… getting to and from school, too. (They don't believe me on that one.) Why I share my stories with them about my history and about what I do now is so they will understand that no matter where we come from we have the power to make better decisions, because our decisions shape our lives. Our habits shape our lives. If we want the best possible future, we have to create good habits and stick with them. To get to our goals means we have to look at things… and the people in our lives… differently. This can be painful, but it is absolutely necessary if we want change to take place.

Developing better habits starts with your peer group.

I don't know about you, but when I was growing up I heard "birds of a feather flock together." Huh? It didn't make a lot of sense then, but I get it now. If I am hanging out with a bunch of slow-moving turkeys it's likely that I too might be a slow-moving turkey. How on earth am I going to learn to fly and feel great about flying by hanging out with these turkeys? That's for the birds! (Okay, enough with the feather-related

analogies.) You want to surround yourself and be around individuals who you most want to replicate. We all have habits, but successful people have a particular set of habits that you need to develop in yourself… In your character.

Again, we all have habits. If yours aren't working to create the success you desire, it's time to change your habits. Change your patterns. I use an example that is easy to embrace in episode #4 of my podcast about dental hygiene. Maybe you brush your teeth. Great. But maybe you want to have better dental hygiene. That means you have to adjust your thinking when it comes to the habit of brushing your teeth. For better dental hygiene you will need to brush longer, brush more thoroughly and brush more frequently, right? You take on those habits and you will have much-improved dental hygiene. So let's take a step into the habits of successful real estate investors. You want to BE that, don't you? Indulge me. I'm going to ask you a few questions.

Would a habit of a real estate investor be, say, writing offers? Would a good habit of a real estate investor be attending networking events? Would a good habit of a real estate investor be to grow a database of contacts and understand which resources he/she has and what the contacts are looking for? Would developing yourself personally and understanding your own emotions – for example, the difference between fear, greed and discipline, and understanding how you respond to these different emotions – be a good thing for you as an investor to know? To be an investor, are there any technical requirements? By that I mean do you need some additional

vocabulary? If so, what is the specialized knowledge – as it says in the book Think and Grow Rich – which you as an investor would need to have to provide solutions to problems that others might bring to you? What are the habits that would benefit you most if you want to be successful not just as a real estate investor but also in life? Would a real estate investor consistently invest in his/her own education beyond any sort of technical skills necessary, to become a better person and to enable him/her to serve more people?

The answer to each question is YES! Yes, yes and yes. To me, these are all habits that a real estate investor must possess, pursue and continue to improve upon. Are these habits you currently practice? No? That's okay. That's the point of being in the process of "becoming." Think of yourself as a caterpillar. You can become a butterfly. To become the best real estate investor you can be will require you to develop better habits. You must embrace the change that is coming.

Change is good. Embrace it!

When we start talking about change, it brings up all kinds of emotions. However, what you might not understand is that the change happens instantly. For example, you're not a smoker until suddenly you are. You decide to make a change, and the next instant you're not a smoker any longer because you don't smoke! It boils down to a decision, which quite literally pushes you to take action immediately. The difference is what you do after you make that decision. Do you stick to the decision and create new habits? What habits do you change to achieve your stated goal?

Let's take another example. One instant you're an employee. The next instant you're self-employed. What is different now is how you go about maintaining your new status. How are you changing the habits that follow your decision? Now let's take this mindset into investing. One moment you're an investor of single-family homes. The next moment you invest in apartment buildings. What has changed? The habits you've developed as an investor in single-family homes that carry over to being an investor in multi-family dwellings! What has changed is your ability to reinforce those habits daily and consistently, so that you eventually become what it is that you are seeking to become right now... a successful real estate investor. Once you have made the decision to BECOME a real estate investor, the next progression is that your thoughts and thought patterns change, your feelings change, and what you believe about yourself and your abilities (or what's holding you back) changes. Next, your activity level, your results, habits, character and then destiny all change. Why? Because all of these things begin to be congruent to align with the new identity that you're developing. To think... it all starts with how you think about things.

Earlier in this section, the topic of developing new habits was discussed. I think you get it by now. So let's talk about the HABIT of writing an offer. This activity is NOT an event. It is part of what you do as a real estate investor. The end. In one of my podcast episodes, I go into this and ask listeners if they know the difference between an event and a common, everyday part of their job as an investor. For example, Christmas is an event because it is something we plan for with great excitement every year. The same can be said about speaking events, which are planned far in advance and take the participation of many people to make them work. I ask listeners if they could imagine if a nurse were to make an event out of drawing blood, administering a medication or connecting an IV to a patient. What I'm saying is that this is not an event any more than your writing an offer is an event. So don't make it a big deal.

A lot of new investors can treat writing an offer like it's an event. It's not. It's the foundation of what you do. You make no money on a property or land (or anything else, for that matter) that you don't control. If you don't control the asset, the asset cannot bring you cash flow. To gain control of the asset, you have to make an offer to purchase the asset. It's pretty simple.

Writing an offer is just an invitation to have a conversation. It's like extending your hand for a handshake. It's like a smile after you say hello. Writing an offer is the beginning of a conversation, yet I've talked to a lot of people who think it is the end of the conversation. Why? Because the offer was refused or they didn't get an immediate yes. Here's the deal... the seller will have at least one concern. Okay? You have to get to that concern.

Think about it like this… Say you write an offer and the seller says yes immediately and with no qualms. Hmmmm… That might mean that you wrote a bad offer for yourself, something that could have been written differently that would bring you more income. Trust me on that one. It's happened to me. I'd rather have a bit of back and forth to get to a final agreement with the seller.

Challenge yourself to change.

You've decided to make a change to your habits and to put a spit-shine on your character. You decided to take aim and fire at new objectives. You know that reading more books on business and real estate investing will help you and that you must meet new people. The question then becomes, "Am I going to read new books and meet new people?" If so, how many new people and how many new books on a monthly/weekly/daily basis?

Here is my rule of thumb: Meet a minimum of five new people each week and read two books a month. (If two is one too many, bump it down to one. The point is to read new books!) This is a fantastic starting point. As you may have gleaned at this point, I meet more than five new people in a week. I don't read as quickly as I like, so I read two or three new books a month. You can track my activity on that side of the fence on my website at www.CashflowDiary.com. If you have book suggestions for me, let me know. There is a quick-link tab that allows you to shoot me an email!

Another technique that I continue to use to this day that helped me develop better habits toward my business is to "trap" myself into success. By trapping yourself into success, you are simply communicating to anyone and everyone about what you plan to do. That's right! I said you TELL people your plans, and yes… it is hard at first. It gets easier and when the people in your life start seeing your plans being implemented into action, they will become believers. For example, you're going to build a website for your new real estate wholesaling business. Great! Tell your family and friends, "Hey, I'm going to create a website." Or, "Hey, I'm going to buy real estate. I'm going to write five offers a week. I'm going to [fill in the blank]."

If people were listening, they'll keep you in check and they'll keep you motivated. They will ask you later, "How's that [fill in blank] going?"

If you are developing better habits and becoming a person of character, action and intent, you will be happy to respond with, "It's going well!" Then you can tell them the process and what is happening with you around your new goals. Congrats! You have successfully trapped yourself into success. Now, keep going.

Another character-building technique that I use involves developing your impact on others. You want to become an influencer in people's lives. So, how does that work? First, you have to understand that you can be impactful and then give thought to the "why" and "how" of this new reality. Your friends want to cheer you on. They want for you the same that you want for you: success. They're looking for someone in their group to be successful, to get behind and ultimately to be able to say, "I know that guy/gal!" I see you shaking your head, but I know I'm right.

Think about it. Have you ever been sitting at your computer or watching a sports event on TV and found yourself cheering for the people you're watching? Sure you have. Why? You like what you see and you want the team to win. You may not have a favorite team. Maybe you tuned into an event between two foreign countries, but something in one of the teams made you stop and watch. Made you pick a side and stick around. Made you cheer. The truth about us as human beings, as spiritual entities, is that we are all looking for someone who will have an impact on us. It is pretty exciting when you become that impactful being. I'm sure you have experienced this on some level in your life. But it didn't happen in a vacuum. You did something that people could see that made you ultimately more interesting… to become someone who was worthy of being cheered on.

Another technique I have used is to find mentors. I didn't just suddenly morph into the real estate investment guy I am today. I didn't just read books and change my habits. I surrounded myself and hung out with those I wanted most to emulate. And I found people who know more than I do about real estate investing. I paid them to mentor me. Why? Because where I was at when I first began as a real estate investor and what was holding me back from true success was a result of

my poor habits. My life was the result of my **best thinking**. Right now you might be saying, "Huh?" It means that everything you are currently experiencing in your life is a result of the "best ideas" you have ever had. These ideas have gotten you where? They have culminated into X, Y and Z, which happens to be what you currently call your life. If you aren't exactly happy with where you are right now in your life, you may not want to take responsibility for where you are currently. One of the steps to changing one's life is to realize and accept that everything that has happened up to this point in your life as an adult is a result of your "best thinking" and implementation of that thinking, plus your skills and techniques. There's a quote I really like that says, "Nobody can go back and start a new beginning, but anyone can start today and make a new ending." It's true.

So, what next? Once you have accepted that just maybe your thinking could be a lot better, it's time to look for mentors and build a board of advisors to help you in making better decisions moving forward. I'll throw in here that I strongly suggest you attend more seminars and events that put you in alignment with people you want to emulate. Learn how these mentors and advisors reached the place you say you want to be. Learn how they think! It's not so much their skills, techniques and the way they do things that is crucial. You will develop your skills. It's how these winners think… their thought processes… that you need to focus on.

As I discuss in the team-building step, we have to be okay with admitting that we don't know everything. We don't have all the answers. We need a team of great advisors that we can depend on who have integrity and character. I cover this in the team-building step, but the people in my team are people I trust big time. I am open to their ideas, and I am not intimidated about asking questions. Hey, I'm all about asking questions. You might have figured that out about me by now.

One final technique I strongly endorse to help you shift your mindset and change your habits to create the life you want is to make the best use of your time. Use it wisely. Redeem your time in a way that helps you continually gain the thought processing of those you wish to be most like.

We truly are spiritual creatures, and as such it is easy to agree that our actions really do matter. Our actions in our lives and our actions in regard to others are very, very important. Yet we see so many times, especially in the worlds of real estate investing and finance, an abundance of greed that doesn't serve the greater good of our fellow man and woman. There is a way to make a good living as a real estate investor while helping people at the same time. It's called "creative financing." That doesn't mean take advantage of people or be a greedy entrepreneur. Quite the contrary.

What's so bad about GREED?

I don't have to tell you that greed is a self-serving mechanism. There are self-servers in this world and there are those who serve others to provide solutions to problems. I never want

to be greedy. That's a choice. Believe me, there is enough real estate and there is enough money to go around. Greed is an off-putting character trait, but I've seen plenty of it. I don't like dealing with greedy people, and I never act in greed. There is nothing good about greed. Or maybe you already know that. (I certainly hope so.) I don't want you to get into real estate investing because you can earn a lot of money. While you certainly can make a fabulous living as a real estate investor, that should not be your driving force. Helping people, leaving a legacy and being a problem solver… those are the reasons to get into real estate investing. If you are doing this as an act of greed I can guarantee you that we will not be working together. If, however, you want to help others and share in my vision, it's quite likely that we can do deals together. As an investor, you'll be dealing with two primary emotions at all times: fear and greed.

You have to learn there are varying degrees of self-control and self-discipline that come into play in any deal. You have fear on one side and you have greed on the other. Every person that would be an investor or would be a business owner is dealing with both of those emotions all the time, every day.

Fear typically shows up when you are looking to buy: "Should I buy, can I buy, will it work, what happens if it all goes bad?" That's when we are thinking of all the reasons why we shouldn't do something.

Greed happens when you are looking to sell. When you have something that is of value and you think someone is going to

try and take advantage of you because they want a different price and you are focused on those things. Greed makes you hold on for more and think, "If I wait I can get another $10." Greed isn't a good trait, but both greed and fear play into a lot of different decisions. Greed plays into capitalism, too, which has become a dirty word. However, capitalism can be a good force if used properly. I call it "cooperative capitalism."

When you think about what competition is (that you are afraid that someone is going to take what is yours), it's what you focus on. That way of thinking comes from a mindset of limitation or scarcity – like there is not enough, which is not true. Everything that has been made could be made again and there is more than enough for all of us. In fact, there is too much for some people. My point is that when you are talking about greed and fear, you have to understand that they both destroy you from the inside. These emotions are not always easily detected in real estate investors. You have to train your ears to hear the fear and greed. For example, when people are afraid they might say, "I don't know how to do that" or "I have never done that" or "But I am new." The reason we say, "I am new," is because we are very self-focused. In a real estate transaction, we think the whole thing depends on us. If you are new and think everything in a deal is dependent on you, yeah, that's a problem.

"New" sends me to a whole new level of irritation, because that is just the easiest excuse that people give to not get involved in anything. As one of my mentors used to say, "When you are afraid, any excuse will do." That is the truth,

and the excuse we will give if we want to get out of something will be the easiest for others to accept, especially if those others are family and friends. That's why environment is so deadly! If our friends are willing to accept the excuse, they will also validate the excuse.

I've met people who have never "overcome" a problem. They have made the problem insurmountable in their minds. When I encounter someone like this, it only makes me push harder for answers. Sometimes after I've pushed to get a person to see that nothing is really holding them back except themselves, the individual will tell me, "Well, J., you don't know my situation!" Indeed I don't, but my question then becomes, "Has anyone ever been in your situation and overcome it?" That takes people by surprise. (Remember that I believe in not-so-gentle Carefrontation™!) If the answer to my question is YES, then the excuse is not valid. Just because you never overcame something doesn't mean you won't ever overcome it. This is just fear holding you back.

You are afraid to face your situation and actually deal with the consequences of what would happen if you did. You know what the true definition of the word "decision" is? It means "to cut off" as in you are making a conscious choice to cut off other options and you will do what it takes to make the option you are choosing happen. Most people don't make decisions, because A) they don't cut off and B) they don't do what it takes to make what they just decided to do actually happen. A decision is both mental and physical. You must make the decision and then you must take steps to see that decision through.

When I am afraid, that means I'm making a decision to cut off the possibility of prosperity, hope, future, abundance and anything else that might be good in favor of something that for whatever reason I have said is of greater value at this moment or at least in that decision. The same thing happens on the greed side! When you are greedy you cut off the same possibilities. When you are feeling greedy you are trying to take advantage of the other party in some way, shape or form. You are violating the fundamental rule of business. You give more in "use" value than you take in cash value.

Want an example? Okay. Say I meet an original American Indian who for some reason is lost in time and still living on the land like in the old west days. He uses his knife and really lives off the land. He has some very valuable furs and I give him an iPad in exchange for some of them. He can get all the furs he wants very easily. I know there are people back in California that are going to pay hundreds, if not thousands of dollars for these things. Yet I give him an iPad. If I do this, I'm acting in greed, and I am taking advantage of him because he has absolutely no use for the iPad. You might say, "But that's worth a lot of money, too." That's irrelevant! He has no use for it, and I have taken more from him in "cash value" than I gave him in use value, and that is a problem. It doesn't have to be an equal exchange, but there has to be a fair exchange. "Win-win" does not mean equal, but there has to be a fair exchange on both sides of the trade.

Greed and the Cashflow Quadrant...

Let's talk about greed in the work sector. In Robert Kiyosaki's Cashflow Quadrant, we see employees, self-employed, business owners and investors. In the employee and self-employed or small business owner quadrants, the primary theme of the day is the word "I." Employees are thinking things like how many hours must I work, when do I get vacation and what are my benefits? Employees are on the take more than they are *on the give.* Self-employed people are thinking typically "I make this much per hour; this is my rate." They value their time very highly, which is fine, but that's their primary motivation. They have to be greedy to a certain extent. In the other two quadrants, business owner and investor, you'll find people to be more "others-focused." If you want to own a business or be a successful investor you must be focused on others' needs. You can't be greedy to make things work well. If you want to grow a business of any means or size you have to focus on the biggest problem and how to solve it. Instead of an "I" mentality, it shifts to a "we" mentality. "We can solve together and by doing so we benefit hundreds if not millions of people." It could just be bottled water. If I alone produce bottled water, it is only going to be one bottle every week. Conversely, if we produce bottled water, we can ship hundreds of thousands of bottles of water to stores every day and solve the problem of making water convenient for many people!

My point is that the thought process of the person at the top of an organization is what matters, because the company's

identity comes from the top. That person's identity is reflected across the entire business. It is a reflection of leadership. When you work with people in a business, are they generous or are they mostly concerned about losing their job? Do they feel empowered to make a decision? Are they greedy? Investors are looking at you as someone who does real estate deals exactly the same. They don't want to see a Greedy Gus. They want to know how much good their money can do. Of course, "good" is a relative term. For some people good could mean cigarettes. They think investing in a cigarette company is a good deal and they choose to invest. That's their investor identity. If you choose to help them in that goal, well, that is your choice. The point is that you are looking to solve the challenges of many people. That's what I love about the business of real estate. Solving the problems! I was taught that the bigger the problem the bigger the solution, and the bigger the solution the more money there is to be earned. So I look for problems... big ones. That's why apartment buildings appeal to me more than single-family homes.

When I say that, I am not just talking about the number of units in an apartment complex and how I can solve the problem of tenants needing a place to live. I'm talking way bigger than that! For example, depending on the size of your apartment complex, it can actually change that entire zip code. I mean that you can make a positive impact in an entire zip code by making improvements to a sizable apartment complex. It is not just about, yeah, we provide 200 doors or 180 doors or 400 doors at this location. That's great, but beyond the 200 doors we are creating four or five consistent jobs on the

property alone. Then you create other jobs and opportunities for so many more people, like the cable company laying in new cable, the construction team helping you put in the new day care center and the additional people required to run your operations. If you are the leader at the top of your organization, this is the successful mindset to take on. What can WE do together to affect change (not how can I make more money)? This is the approach we (my team and I) take with every investment deal.

Look at improvements in a new way.

When my team and I look at apartment complexes, we might see a great deal of wasted common area. Maybe the owners have been too lazy to do something about it or haven't thought about it, but it interests me to see all that usable space going unused. I immediately start thinking about how we use that area instead of just paying property taxes on it. We actively seek out those types of complexes now. We know we've found a good one if the playground isn't being used and the space is right for something more useful. Maybe we can put in a day care center or maybe a car wash. I don't know. What could we add that would bring more value? We can't just let the space go to waste. Adding something of value will bump up the profit, and there is nothing wrong with earning a profit, especially if we are being socially conscious at the same time.

In being socially conscious, my team and I will not be greedy. We won't violate someone's trust. We will only participate

in deals of fair trade. And I don't want anything "for free." I want to earn it, whatever that "it" happens to be. I may earn it by negotiating well, which is a fair exchange because if you are paying attention during the negotiation, well then, I just taught you how to be a better negotiator. But that's the problem. Not a lot of people are paying attention these days. They want things done for them so they don't have to do whatever it is they want done themselves. That's fine, too. If you can pay someone else to do something for you, go ahead. But then don't complain that you don't know how to do it. If that is how you think, if you don't want to learn new skills that are necessary in doing real estate deals, then that's why you don't have the skill set already. You're probably really good at making excuses for your behaviors or why you don't do things, too, right? Maybe you say that you have too much "chaos" in your life to hunker down and study or to take the steps necessary to learn new skills.

News flash: Chaos is not holding you back.

Ah, chaos! You enter my home and you'll see a very active toddler running around, exploring his world and trying adventurous new things, like jumping on the couch. He's exploring language and loves the word "hi"! My young son keeps us busy. You could call it chaos. That's fine. I don't let it keep me from accomplishing a great many things. If I can't get things done in my home, I always have the option of heading to Starbucks. I can control the chaos in my head, and so can you. Just like how I suggested that you deal with your fear, it

is your response to chaos that makes a difference in your life. Choose to keep a cool head always.

You know what I think? Where there is TRUE chaos, there is cash flow! Stick with me. How can you say that, J.? Because the chaos is fear in disguise! Where there is fear, there is a problem to be fixed. Let's break this down. Say I'm a busy mom and I am afraid to participate in real estate. I have anxiety about making mistakes or the process, so instead of saying I'm afraid, I say, "Oh, my God, I have 12 soccer games to take all the kids to and clearly I have to be there for my kids! I just don't have time to X, Y or Z."

Wouldn't it be more truthful to say, "You don't want me to sacrifice being there for my kids so that I can actually take on my life and be an example for my kids, do you?"

It's easier to get a job and work for someone else. Being an entrepreneur is frightening for some people. You get to use the chaos excuse. There is chaos at work and you are needed. There is chaos at home, so you can't find time to make changes in your life. All you have to do is show up when "they" tell you to and do just enough work to keep you from getting fired, and you get paid just enough so that you don't quit. It all becomes a mutually destroying symbiotic relationship. Then one day, you wake up and wonder what happened to your life and why didn't you achieve anything. The answer is that you never started. You let whatever chaos get in the way.

Let's talk about that for a minute. What is your definition of chaos? A dirty house? Do you really, really have to clean the house? Do you let distractions get cha? I mean, do you really have to watch Dexter? Do you really have to? Don't get me wrong, I like to watch *So You Think You Can Dance, Glee*, and *Shark Tank*. I will take some time to watch those shows. I am not saying don't do these things. What I am saying is that you need balance. Balance the things you do against the things you should be doing to get you further ahead in life. Let's say I give you a magic scale. On one side you can put weight toward your dreams and the other side toward more chaos. Which side of the scales is lower right now? What I'm saying is that you can continue to make decisions that reinforce bad habits (remember our discussion about habits?) that keep adding weight to the chaos side or you can start making better decisions on the other side.

Fear, chaos and elderly investors.

We can talk all we want about adding to our chaos scale, but we don't know what real chaos is. Elderly investors lived through true chaos, for example, if they were alive in 1929. Bad year for paper assets investors! (Not so much for those who held land and property.) Those who lived through the Stock Market Crash and the Great Depression may have some fixed ideas around investing. You will have to work a little harder to get them to be open to hearing about your vision.

The Great Depression tainted millions against the whole concept of risk and they became penurious savers. They were some of the best savers on the planet because they understood that tomorrow they may not have food, money, home or anything else. They were good stockpilers of canned goods, too. They learned what it meant to survive. They learned that to survive meant to save. Save what? Everything! Reuse the clothes, reuse the shoes, sew that sole back on, make your own dress… everything. If they didn't they would not survive. Talk about adapt or die! This was a very real concept to that group of individuals.

The difference now is that to survive (because the rules of money have changed), you must learn to invest. Saving is the riskier move. Investing is actually the safer move when you are in an inflationary and more hyper-inflationary environment. However, real estate investing is a better way to go in my humble opinion for lots of reasons. If you don't understand paper investing, here's a quick crash course…

Real estate vs. traditional paper investments.

When it comes to investing money, it's all about control. Who controls your investment and why are we so willing to give up control? That comes down to not understanding how control works. With investments outside of real estate the control is in the hands of others. As a real estate investor, you retain control of your money and your future. Here's what I mean…

When you invest in the stock market, you are investing in companies. Let's say you find a company you really want to invest in. Great. It can work. You can gain good returns. Popi and I have invested in stocks and have done well. Just like in the Cashflow game, my wife found a great low-priced stock and bought as much as she could. Then it skyrocketed in price and she sold for a very tidy profit. That's the way to do it! But it's not something you can count on and it isn't something you can really control. If you want control as a stockholder, you'd have to own a controlling interest in the stock you are buying. You have to influence the Board of Directors for that company. Conversely, real estate investing gives you full control over the deal. You affect the outcome through your actions and decisions.

Mutual funds by law can't do certain things. They cannot go to cash. Compare that model with the real estate market. Some real estate investors saw danger coming. They had control and could take action. By that I mean they had the choice to sell properties. With mutual funds, that's not possible. Once your money is tied up in mutual funds and the money managers are managing FOR YOU, you've lost control. You get to take the ride all the way down. Life savings and nest eggs have been lost just like that.

Hedge funds don't give you control either. The reporting isn't there. But I'm not going into how you gather and use hedge funds here. I can use hedge funds in real estate deals, but I don't do a lot of that.

Bonds may be a safer bet. In the real estate world, it's akin to "holding notes." Traditional bonds are based on a promise of a company. Fixed assets are sometimes not valued correctly. You don't have control. In real estate where you hold the notes, you have control.

With traditional forms of paper investing, there is little to no downside protection, unless you know how to properly use options or other derivatives. And insider trading is a big no-no. In real estate, however, insider trading is not only a good thing, but rather it's preferred. Real estate is based on it! The communication and sharing of information about properties and deals is crucial to one's success in real estate investing. It is a good thing to be the one who is "in the know," but it also takes more work to get to that position.

The major difference between paper asset investing and real estate is the interpersonal skills and relationships. Real estate investors need these skills. What I like in my Cash Flow Creation System (check it out on my website) is that it teaches skills of building and using interpersonal skills. To go out there into the world to do good in the community, to build hospitals and day care centers and youth centers takes a whole lot of interpersonal skills. That's my goal, and I continue building my skills every day. It never stops. If we want to work with Hope Worldwide to build hospitals in third-world countries, we need interpersonal skills to get the ball rolling and then we need a whole bunch of other people to see our vision and help us reach the goal.

Real estate provides shelter, which is a basic human need. Every building, every home, every restaurant, every movie theatre is built on something. It's called land. You invest in land where people will one day be and you will be there to provide the shelter and entertainment outlets once they arrive. But that takes some research on your part. We'll get to that. I don't need stock. I need a place to live, work, play and lay. Even when I pass from this world, I am going to need a bit of real estate to rest (to lay) eternally. You ARE participating in real estate even if you're not investor. Think about it. If you rent, you participate in real estate because you're paying a landlord. If you own your home, you participate in real estate because you are paying a mortgage company. If you go to your favorite movie theatre, guess what? You're participating in real estate. Someone owns that business and the land it's built on.

Real estate provides benefits beyond what paper assets can give you. For example, real estate brings political favor and tax incentives. Do mutual funds? Stocks? No. Real estate investing is embraced by government officials. I may not like it, but it's a fact. Politicians will not be elected a second time if they don't get involved with housing in their districts.

Regarding interest deductions on your taxes, I'll leave the nitty gritty to your tax professional, but real estate gives you opportunity for such deductions. The government gives us tax incentives to buy real estate and to improve it. There is a reason the government decided to float Fanny and Freddie. These entities are still very much in operation, and it's not to make a profit. Again, I am not going to go into the minutia

here about this topic. That's not what this book is about. What I hope you get from my information is that there are many reasons to invest in real estate vs. other forms of investing.

There is no greater access to other people's money than through real estate. Why? Because there is proof of concept with real estate investing. By that I mean that in real estate there is already proof that it exists, it is needed and it is valuable. It is up to us to decide that value and to trade on that value, but the need for real estate has been proven for thousands of years. The same cannot be said of a new business idea or an invention. In those you must prove over and over the concept behind the business or goods or service. Investors need to be shown that the business idea will work or the new gadget you've invented will sell like hot cakes before they put their money on the table. It's a challenge to get a new business funded even when you have a great idea. The days of easy access to venture capital are long gone. Ask a broker whose task it is to find money for even the most solid business models and new gadgets.

In real estate there is a specific tax code that you should familiarize yourself with if you are serious about investing. It's tax code section 179 in which the government allows an investor in real estate to get paid but not actually "earn" any money. This code is built around DEPRECIATION of the property, and allows you to write off pieces of the property's value over time. I am not a tax expert, but I can tell you that this is something you want to check with your tax professional about when you start doing more and larger real estate deals.

You need to learn some of the basic laws that affect your taxes as a real estate investor. I'm not telling you to take a course in tax law. I'm just saying you need to be aware of your rights, the benefits and the possible penalties. For example, did you know that you can actually incur penalties for flipping a property you've held? It's called capital gains. If you sell and then reinvest your gains into other properties in a certain time frame, that is far better than paying a penalty on the monies you just earned. That's right. It's earnings. Additionally, you should eventually familiarize yourself with something called Cost Segregation where you can depreciate parts of building faster than other parts. For example, it could take 27 ½ years in a residential property to adequately depreciate items and 39 years for commercial property. That means you can use the money more in the beginning, which benefits you in the long-term. This is a more complicated deal structure and something you can tackle later. For now, keep it simple and work your way up. Don't get overwhelmed. You will be developing a team of people who will all be responsible for different aspects of the deals.

Here's the point. You cannot do any of these things with annuities and other paper asset investments. Maybe investing in the stock market is great for the average person. How about this…. DON'T BE AVERAGE!

I want you to get beyond the "I can't succeed in real estate because…" mentality. If you think this is true, it's only true because you THINK it is. So stop it. Bother to learn about

political and tax incentives that will put more money into your pocket with your real estate investments.

You want to know another advantage of investing in real estate vs. paper assets? Leverage! As an example, I can buy something that appreciates in value over time with no money down and no credit of my own in real estate. I cannot do the same with, let's say, a life insurance policy or an annuity. Hey, wars have been fought over real estate. I figure that says a lot about how good of an investment it might be, right? What is war if not extreme chaos, but in such times who wins out? That's right. Those who own real estate.

Real estate investing gets us through true chaos.

I have friends from Estonia who experienced communism and a lot of true chaos. Their words ring in my head even today, because what they say is true. It has always been true. They said the people who were okay during the chaotic, uncertain times were those who owned real estate and had a business. It was the bread line for those who didn't.

If to survive meant jumping up and down, we would be a culture that jumped up and down all day. That's because none of us wants to die; we will do what it takes to live. For the Great Depression babies, saving simply meant life. Now things are different. Saving isn't the right path. Investing is the correct thinking. We should talk about this more in society and educate people more about investing. Unfortunately, no one has created a campaign called "Investing Is Life." But it is. That message hasn't come completely clear yet. It will one day, but it will become very clear and a bit late for many as a result of some cataclysmic economic failure. (Look at other countries in the news.) Then people will say, "Uh, oh. My money is worthless. Now what do I do? I don't have anything that can generate money, whatever that new money is. I'm in trouble!"

Truth is that we as a country are in trouble. If something happens to completely devalue the dollar, it means that stockpile of cash you've been hoarding turns into a stockpile of valueless paper that is only good as a source of heat. I don't keep a lot of cash. Remember, I'm an investor. Those who know me might ask me why. I am not a doom-and-gloom guy, but the truth is that I could wake up tomorrow and my dollars are worthless, but my real estate still has value! It has "utility value" and if I suddenly need sheep, guess what? I can house the shepherd and he will give me sheep. Keeping with this line of thinking, maybe I'll need someone who also knows how to shear the sheep. I certainly don't have that skill; I have to find the person who knows how to shear the sheep. When I do, I'd ask him if he'd like a place to stay. Yes, he would. I'd say, "Cool, and here is your job. You are going to shear the sheep that the shepherd is going to provide." Awesome. Because I have real estate, I've given two men and their families a place to live in trade for something of value that will help me feed my family.

The next step in this hypothetical story would be that I'd need to find a tailor. That shouldn't be a problem, because guess

what that tailor needs? Yep. A place to stay. You get my point. I chose this example because clothing has a universal value. Everyone needs clothes. Maybe people don't need clothes all the time; not everyone needs sheep all the time; not everybody needs a sheep shearer all the time; however, everyone needs a place to stay. If I am the provider of the place to stay, then whatever I accept or am willing to accept in exchange for allowing people the use of my place, then it is a symbiotic and mutually beneficial relationship. That's where the term landlord comes from. A few centuries back, you got to live, work, play and lay in a place owned by the landlord. In return, you made food. It was a fair trade. A landlord (a real lord in this case, as in king of the castle) would say something like, "I have land. But since you don't have land, how about I let you use some of my land for some of your food? You have to give me 25% of the food you create. Now, I don't need 25% of the food, so I will end up with a stockpile of food. Yes, you have to do the work and I get to sit on my throne waiting for you to deliver my 25%. You can't get mad at me because I have land." Okay, I took a few liberties here with the language, but you get what I'm saying. This was in a time before everyone had the right to own land. Farmers (peasants) had the right to be upset that they weren't allowed to own land. But now that we have property rights and you can be a property owner, what is your excuse?

Use chaos to your advantage as an investor.

In the external world, chaos is opportunity. I look for it. For example, a distressed property owner is in chaos. I can

certainly help him/her. News is chaos, too. I don't listen to
the news, but I do listen to the financial and federal policy
updates. What I'm really doing is looking for opportunities!
I keep an eye on the financial and real estate news, because
that's where I can find opportunities in real estate. However,
I see those types of opportunities in other areas of the news,
too. I call this taking a dip (or for us investors... "DIIP") into
the news... DIIP News. It's short for a process that I use to find
opportunities in my local paper. Here it is... my process in a
nutshell:

I will take an article from an online paper (news distribution
channel) and break it down to find the nuggets of opportunity.
Let's just say I'm on MSNBC and we're going to travel back in
time to June 15th, 2012. The headline of one article caught my
eye. It read, "Million-dollar earners making a comeback, tax
returns show." You're asking, "Okay, so what does that have
to do with me?" Hang on. As a real estate investor looking
for opportunities, it should make your investor senses tingle.
You're looking for clues. Success leaves clues. (I took that from
Tony Robbins, and he is correct.) Where do the clues take us in
this article?

Let's look at the information in this article that states "the
number of million-dollar earners fell 40% in the financial
industry meltdown and great recession of 2007 to 2009 before
making a comeback in 2010, the most recent year available."
The article went on to state that "in 2010, about 268,000
taxpayers reported adjusted gross incomes of a million dollars

or more, up from 237,000 in 2009. And 237,000 taxpayers in 2009 was a six-year low." Six-year low? Wow. And these millionaires represent just a tiny fraction of the nation's total of 143M taxpayers. (Just a small sliver of the top 1%.) It's about the top 0.2%! What this particular article is giving us is some information about the financial health of our entire United States from the personal-income perspective.

Now, this is what I find so interesting. I kept reading to learn that "while millionaires are making a comeback, this year has been less promising for the millions of people in the middle class." The article went on to say that the nation's median income was reported as being $49,445 in 2010, a decline of 2.3% from 2009 once adjusted for inflation. Hmmm… The average income then would be $49,445.

What this article is telling me is that there are some people who seem to be earning more money. It is also telling me that those in the middle class aren't those people. I ask myself what the millionaire tax returns have in common. So, see, first of all, we've got to go through the D – I – I - P!

Data is the first part of the process. What information you get from most news channels is just a bunch of data! Numbers and facts. In this article it said that "in 2010, 268,000 taxpayers reported an adjusted gross income of $1M or more, up from 237,000 in 2009. This is data. It has no meaning. It's just data.

Information is where we go next. We have to take this data and turn it into information. Numbers quoted in the article are

then followed with a great bit of information: "A six-year low." Now it's time to interpret the data and information.

Interpret the information in the article and you will see that you can become one of these millionaire taxpayers, because what the article says is that someone with a million-dollar adjusted gross income is the definition given for a "millionaire taxpayer." The article also states that these people are married (40% of them anyway) and over the age of 55. That's not me. But that's not what I zoned in on.

Do you think that those individuals could be easily targeted with some of the information that you just now learned? You just learned that you know what their average gross income (AGI) is, you know they're mostly married, and you know that they're typically 55 and older. Could you use that information to figure out what section of town that might be, where most of those individuals are, where they live, etc.? Could you use that information in any way, in your real estate (or any other) business, to help you figure out your next steps in marketing? You'll ask yourself, "Who is it that I want to serve?" Uh, now you have your answer. Hope this helps you.

"But, J., you left out the 'P'."

You might have figured it out, but the "P" is simply for PROCESS. Yes, I know. Brilliant.

But wait. There's more to the DIIP system...

You could probably use another example of DIIP and how to use it to find nuggets of opportunity. Let's say that you see in the news that 10,000 people were just laid off from their jobs at a particular company. What is that? It's data. Now, let's take that to information. By the time you see the news that 10,000 people were laid off, it's already becoming old news. It took a little time for the reporter to gather the data to make his/her report. So the raw data is the XYZ Company just reduced their work force by 10,000 people. From the data, you can now gather the message (the information) that this "bad" thing happened. So, all of these people are losing their jobs. Sad. As a real estate investor, however, you need to look at it another way. You need to interpret the information through different eyes. You know what I think when I see something like that in the news? I'm thinking that I just found 10,000 new leads, because these people might be looking to do something different in their lives! Now what I need to do is come up with an ad that asks, "Did you just get laid off by XYZ Company? Call this number." These are very specific leads that you can market to over time, which is what you need to do to take advantage of the massive opportunity that is before you.

Data to Information to Interpretation. What's next? I place the ad in the newspaper or Craigslist where that happened and guess who calls me; those very people who were frustrated and just got laid off by that XYZ Company. Guess what all of them have? A retirement plan. And now that they are separated from their company… guess what they get to do? Move the plan anywhere they want to. What if all 10,000 of them only have $10,000 each in his/her retirement plan? What if I got 100 of these people? That's a million dollars! And it all came from my reading a news article that was supposedly bad news. The problem is what the news wants you to interpret. The news wants us to believe things are so bad that we have to watch the news to keep up with what's going on to stay safe. I would, but I am too busy dealing with the 10,000 leads I just found. I don't have time to watch the next news segment.

To hammer this point home, sometimes at a seminar I'm leading I will just ask for a newspaper. This is something I can do on any day, in any city, at any time. Someone in the audience will hand me a newspaper. I will flip through and it may not be on the front page, but something in there will tell me that *here is a good customer to serve with real estate*. For example, here is a very morbid but true statement… if you really want to think about real estate for a second, think about the fact that everything the Baby Boomers have ever touched has exploded in growth in terms of need and products and services. When they needed baby food Gerber blew up. When elementary schools were needed construction went through the roof. When they needed housing, that industry went absolutely nuts; suburbs were created. Today, due to the aging Baby Boomer generation, it's medical devices that are blowing up! Retirement destinations are going crazy. Acute care and elder care facilities, too. At some point this generation of people will die. If you are the guy or gal out there right now buying a whole bunch of land and/or currently

underperforming funeral homes, you'll do okay, because more cemeteries and funeral homes are going to be needed. You can spot the trends by looking in the newspaper, too! And let's not forget late-night TV.

I'm guessing that in about 10 years you are going to start hearing on late night TV "How to buy your own funeral home overnight using no money and no credit for just $29.95!" It will be some person who bought today at a very low price and then people will finally see the opportunity. By then it might be too late. This trend will come and go, and then it will get more expensive for people to participate in. Then someone will come up with some insurance policy that pays for all of this stuff. Then it will be time to pay attention to the next trend. At that point, it will be the new Echo boomers – the Baby Boomers' kids who are caught in the "sandwich generation." They'll be trying to figure out what on earth to do with their retirement and they will have their homes paid for, and then what? They will only be served if we real estate investors choose to pass down that information to our kids, so they can serve the people.

Let me bring you back around to the beginning of this discussion. Why did I share all of this about the Boomers? I want you to understand that chaos becomes an indication of the problems that you need to be solving. There are no excuses that work here. There are problems to be solved everywhere. It's your choice to get involved.

Are excuses holding YOU back?

To change your mindset takes courage. It takes some fortitude to say, "You know what? I reject the chaos and excuses; I would rather have [insert good thing here]." You get to hold yourself accountable, because no one is going to hold you accountable in pushing yourself forward. In fact, it is not someone else's responsibility to do so and if you find a group of people who are willing to keep you accountable, then count yourself lucky. Don't let "chaos" and excuses get in your way.

Kids are an easy excuse; I have four of them! Are you kidding? My kids are an easy excuse...a really easy excuse. Spouses are an easy excuse, for example, when I'm talking to a woman about investing and she says, "My husband won't let me." So? I don't care if he won't let you. What does that mean when you tell me he or she won't let you? If that's where you are, you and your significant other have other issues that you need to deal with. I can understand that you may want to do it WITH your spouse. That totally makes sense to me. However, your spouse is not required for you to be successful. Or are you going to tell me that you are going to be happy thinking, "I could be doing this, but my husband/wife won't let me"? Or "I could be doing this and having this and we could be going here, but he/she won't let me." How long is it going to be before you end up resenting your spouse? Not long, because you are going to be thinking about all the stuff that you could have accomplished if it weren't for this person. (Especially when they do something boneheaded and tick you off, right?)

Often we are too afraid to express our desires and live exactly the way we want. We are too afraid to take a stance. So we call it chaos. Unfortunately, our immediate circle of friends are living in the same disguise. They are living in that same bubble, if you will. They reinforce the belief. As a result, we don't push ourselves to become more. We can think, "It's got to be okay just to have a job. After all, Frank has a job and Mary has a job, and they seem okay." Yeah, but Frank is upset all the time, and Mary hates Frank right now because she wishes she could go start a business. Or what she'd really love to do is paint or express herself differently. But she is stuck in a job where she doesn't really have to make decisions about her life. Don't get me wrong. I know that some people actually like what they do in their jobs and that's great. But that does not describe most people. Take me, for example. I was a horrible employee; it took me 26 some odd years to figure that out!

I think if we ever sat down and explained the Cashflow Quadrant to people (for example, when they're in high school) and told them about the pros and cons of each of the quadrants (employee, self-employed, business owner and investor), we would have a radical revolution on our hands. Some people would still choose to be employees and that's great. The world needs employees. At least there wouldn't be so many false expectations. Employees would understand their role and that they have limited options. But what about VPs and CEOs? They are still employees. They just have more zeros and commas in their paychecks. It is harder for them to leave their jobs, because they can't so easily be replaced. It is easier to find a replacement for a $20-an-hour worker. The higher-level executives have to hold on even tighter to their jobs, because they won't so easily find another comparable job. And they get focused on the money they earn... the greed. They know that there is not going to be another CEO job at a Fortune 500 company that they can claim, so they'll hold on tight to their current position. Their mindset is "I'd better get all I can right now." That's called greed.

In this situation, capitalism takes the blame, but that is not capitalism in its truest form. For most people, if they didn't grow with the company or if they weren't a founder of the company it means they were simply hired by the company as a manager. That's all they are. Managing an aspect of the company is their job. In short, they are managing for the shareholders. They may be high up on the food chain in their profession, but these executives are still W-2 employees.

Even professional athletes are W-2 employees. They receive regular paychecks just like other employees. They just happen to work for a company called the San Antonio Spurs or the Los Angeles Angels of Anaheim (or any number of other teams). They are paid for their expertise on the court or in the field just as the executives are paid for their expertise in their professions. They are paid for their time. Wouldn't it be better to value our time vs. being paid for our time?

Learn to value your time!

An old friend gave me a clock years ago. I love this clock! Instead of numbers for the hours, it has dollar values! I don't

know where he found it, but this cool clock breaks down every minute into dollar increments. At the 12 o'clock position it shows "$500," which means I shouldn't spend an hour unless I make $500, right? I had to learn that I can spend my time doing something myself or I can hire somebody to do it cheaper than it costs me to be the person doing that task.

That clock is actually responsible for a lot. It shifted my mindset to help me see time AS money. Time truly is money, you know? The clock came as a result of a very interesting conversation I had at my J - O - B several years back. I was telling a co-worker at the insurance place where I used to put in time that I wanted to hit $20,000 a month in sales. Someone that overheard me said something that rings in my head even today. I forget the man's name, but what he said was simple and profound. He asked me, "Have you ever done that?" I said, "Uh, no." The guy looked at me square in the eyes and said, "How about you learn how to make $2,000 first?" I said, "Good point. I will go do that." Then I was forced to go and think in realistic terms about how I would achieve that goal.

I had to break down the process. If I want to earn $20,000 a month, I have to start somewhere smaller. So how do I earn $2,000? Then how do I work up to ten times that in the same month? That's the simpler breakdown process, which keeps you from short-circuiting yourself. That's what I was doing by putting that large figure in my head! It was such a quantum leap to that number from where I was that my brain couldn't make sense of it. It was by backing off that number and taking baby steps that eventually got me to the number I wanted.

Like I said about the computer programming, I had to learn how to look at my goals in steps. That and I had to learn to rely on other people to help me get to my numbers. I learned that it takes a team to get me to my goals!

STEP SIX:

Develop a Team Game Plan

"There is no limit to what a man can do or where he can go if he doesn't mind who gets the credit." Ronald Reagan

I am really skill set driven. Why? I see that skill sets are what the real estate game is all about! Technically, since time began, the skills to transact real estate have always been highly valued. What has changed is how real estate is transacted and who can own it. We all made an agreement that everyone can buy and sell real estate. Long ago, before the new rules were in place, to transact real estate meant you jumped in your ship and sailed to the neighboring country. You took your army, burned everything down and claimed the land as yours. Ta-da! You got a new piece of land.

Today we are little more civil, and we have title companies and all this other stuff that helps us to transact the exchange of property. We don't necessarily need an army with swords

and catapults to go get more land. Knowing how to transact real estate deals has been a very marketable skill for a very long time. It's a skill that has always been valuable, is valuable today and – unlike most skills – will never become worthless. Why did I just say that? A lot of skills are great for today, but they won't be valuable tomorrow. Let's take typing, for example. There was a time where very few people knew how to type. That's reasonable, because there was a time when there was no typewriter. But when the typewriter came along, we all eventually needed to learn to type. Since there weren't personal computers, there would be entire rooms devoted to typing and typists in a business. For some, that was their job… to type all day… in triplicate! Who knows what they were typing, right? It was a valuable skill. But not so much today, because a whole lot of people type, we have personal computers, smart pads and phones that have full texting capability. Today we have two-year-olds who know how to type! It is nothing for my toddler son to use the keyboard and an iPhone or iPad. He knows how to use these devices. It is not a mystery to him. He doesn't get weighed down by techno-anxiety. He doesn't know a world without a keyboard. For that matter, you know what the lost skill is now? Handwriting is becoming a lost skill! (A lot of people, especially those who are in high school and younger, don't use handwriting. They use block letters. People my age use a combination of block letters and cursive.)

My point is that times change. Mindsets change. Opportunities expand with your base of knowledge and with the people you hang out with. There has never been such an excellent

time to be an entrepreneur! There are so many opportunities, especially in real estate, that it almost boggles the mind. If you can change your mindset to that of an entrepreneur and then develop your leadership skills and gather a team of like-minded people, you'll come out the winner.

Real estate investing is a team sport!

I could get nothing done without my team. I will now repeat that just in case they are reading this or you missed it. I could get nothing done without my team. And I am grateful for their dedication to our vision and to me. Notice I said "our vision." That's what it is… a shared vision, a shared goal. When I brought them onto the team, each of them saw the vision clearly. They each bring a specialty skill to the table. They have my back and I have theirs!

In an early episode my podcast, I cover teamwork. The title of that podcast, in case you want to give it a listen, is "Teamwork Makes the Dream Work." No truer statement can be made. The composition of your team will change as you progress as a real estate investor, and you will definitely need a more experienced one as you do more and more deals, and as your deals become more complicated over time. For example, we just closed a huge deal on a commercial property and I couldn't have done that size of a deal without my team. I grew my business and adjusted my goals to what I'm doing now in these sizable deals! In my team, we each have our role, which makes the process a whole lot smoother. I first imagined (some may say I was delusional) that I would be doing this on my own. Today that idea is utter folly. In fact when someone approaches me and asks for counsel or coaching within their business (real estate-related or otherwise), usually part of the solution is in helping them look at their lack of having access to the right team member(s). Besides, what fun would that be anyway to go on this journey alone? Who is on your team, their character and their clearly defined functions will be imperative to your success. When you have a team, it's not just your success that matters, but rather it becomes the success of your team. A team that is not cohesive in its actions and goals will not be successful.

Think about teams you've seen that miss the mark in what they are trying to achieve. For example, maybe your favorite football team isn't doing so well, but when you look at the team dynamics you see that something is off. Maybe some of the members were traded and the new players haven't yet accepted their roles or they aren't communicating well with the seasoned players of that team. There is some reason why that team isn't playing up to snuff. The teamwork is missing! Once that's fixed you see your favorite team hitting goal after goal, right?

We hit our goals because we communicate!

In our team we have a system in place so that there are no misunderstandings. For any conference call (i.e., distance negotiations, property viewings, decisions to be made) with

an associate or really anyone, we as a team immediately have a follow-up call to go over details of that first call to avoid any miscommunications. We address what is good and bad in the prior call. This system developed as a matter of common sense. We need to make sure everyone is on the same page in a deal. Since language plays a function, we have to make sure we're all speaking the same language (remember the differences in language between the attorney and CFO and other professionals may vary). All of this takes good listening skills on the part of every person on the call. I learned to listen closely to people because the words they use are important. Sometimes the words being used carry a deeper inference. From any good marriage or relationship book you'll learn that the same word may have a different meaning to different individuals. For example, "clean" the kitchen may mean something more to you than it might to me. To me, maybe "clean" means put the dishes in the sink and throw out the garbage. To you that is not enough.

Learning to listen to words and working with a team we have to make sure we are very clear. We want to make sure our words are meaning the same thing to every member on the team. Clarity lends itself to power. Miscommunication is the devil's playground. Again, there is no room for miscommunication.

Why does all this matter so much? I am responsible for millions of dollars, the work environment and the living quarters of many families. I must be sincere in my words. We all should be sincere, even in our everyday communications.

For example, how often has someone asked you how you are and you answered, "Fine." That person didn't care and you probably didn't either. How often have you asked how someone is doing just because it seemed like the thing to do? Did you REALLY listen for the answer? Did you care? Why bother asking if you don't care? At the end of the day, business is nothing but a series of agreements. Being sincere and setting boundaries is a good thing. These things lead to greater clarity. Without clarity my team couldn't do its job. We have to do what we say we are going to do in each and every deal. If I as the leader of the team don't act correctly, how can I expect the team to have correct thinking?

Leadership isn't something that just comes magically to you. It's something that is developed in you over time. My first experiences in life, living in a military family, gave me the leg up on leadership skills, but that is because I had to be a great follower first. And I had to listen a lot. I took that with me out into the world when I started working, too. I learned that everyone has an opinion. To make it I would have to consider other people's ideas and not just stick to my own. That's where my team comes in!

Who should you put on your team?

By this point in the book you might have figured out a few of the professionals you'll need on your dream team. For example, if you end up with a mortgage on a property you may need a good loan officer. If you arrange private financing,

you might need a lender AND a servicing agent who can service the loan to receive and process your payments. You might need a property manager to watch over the hens in the hen house. (These are otherwise referred to as tenants in your rental properties!) Who watches the property manager? Uh, that's your job. I like to draw this simple graphic in my classes to show the monitoring pyramid, if you will:

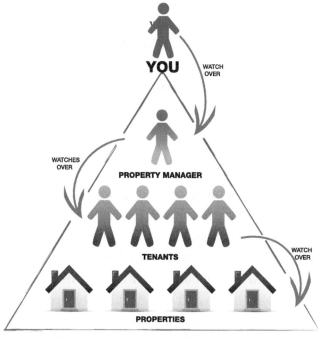

CHAIN OF CASH FLOW COMMAND:
You watch over the Property Manager who watches over the Tenants who watch over your rental properties!

Next you might add a person to handle your insurance, because insurance issues will come up, especially in apartment buildings. Remember my twice-burned building? Those fires resulted in more than a year of insurance issues, but it brought me a lot of good relationships, so I really can't complain. The long and short of having an insurance manager is to make sure that all the properties in your portfolio are well-protected. On your team, you might include a housing inspector, termite inspector and/or general pest-control person (or company), a good real estate agent, cleaning crew, a real estate attorney who is in the know about SEC rules, and you might need a great bookkeeper. On your internal team as your organization grows, you will want to add a very competent Chief Financial Officer (CFO) and even a Vice President of Operations (VPO). I have one of each and I adore these people! First, because they are decent, honest, hard-working individuals; second, because they make my life easier by making deals go as smoothly as possible. I have come to depend greatly on these people for their skills and knowledge.

My CFO isn't just someone who is good at balancing budgets and doing accounting and bookkeeping tasks. This person helps me think on a higher level in financial transactions and more strategically to help me achieve my cash flow and income goals. My VPO handles my operations functions and all the data that goes in and out. At this level I really, really need this person. As your portfolio grows and you see just how much data comes in between the first and the fifth or the first and the 15th of every month, you will understand what I am saying fully. Your VPO puts systems in place to make your operations a lot more simplified and streamlined. With this individual's help, you can continue providing top-quality customer care to everyone you're involved with in a deal, from tenants to top investors. It would be too much for me at

this point to handle all of these duties on my own. I did in the beginning, but that was then and this is now!

Even before your portfolio of properties expands, you should be keeping your eye out for competent people with whom you can work. Keep notes. Make lists. Save their information. Then you will be ready to take the next step, which is the interview. If you're smart, you'll continually interview people as the opportunity presents.

I don't formally interview everyone. Like everything else in my world, finding the right team members starts with a simple conversation. No matter what role the person is to fill, here is what I say (in this case, it's a property manager I'm talking to):

"Hi, my name is J. and I have a property on 123 Main Street that's currently under contract for me to purchase. I'd like to sit down and talk with you to see if you are open to being able to manage it… and manage it in the way that works with my organization."

Other investors might do things differently, but I prefer that there be a deal under contract as I go forth and build the team. There's no real right or wrong way to go about the process. My point is that you need a team when you start doing more deals and more complicated deals. Just be prepared.

There is something else I want you to be prepared for and to understand the importance of, and that is being the weakest link in your team. You need to be the weakest link! That way, your team learns to come up with solutions to problems. You don't have to be THE problem-solver in the group. You gathered this team because they have each proven themselves competent and intelligent problem-solvers, so why not let them put their talents to use? All I have to do is say, "Sounds great!" (If it really does sound great. I don't want you to just blindly agree to anything.) Besides, do you really know everything? Like insurance… do you know as much about insurance issues as someone who is trained specifically to deal with insurance issues? Probably not. Same goes for contracts. Do you know everything about real estate contracts? The beauty is that you don't have to. There are people for that!

Choose offensive and defensive players.

When looking at people to put on your team, you're looking for two types of people. Either they will be put in the role of protecting money or growing money. I like sports references, so let's say that some people play offense in your company and some people play defense. My CFO is a defensive player. You'll see the defensive people inside your organization easily because you see their effect in your company through decreased expenses. That's what should happen: decreased expenses, faster execution and greater operational efficiencies. That's how you'll know the defensive players are doing their job. If they don't show up in one of these three areas, fire them because they are not providing value.

Offensive players are the people doing your marketing

and sales. Clearly this one is going to be obvious, right? You should be able to see the offensive players' effect in increased marketing reach or increased brand recognition, increased sales, increased revenue, etc. Increasing numbers of opportunities should be coming your way. If those things aren't happening, fire these players. Find new ones. They are not the right people. You hired them to increase results across marketing and sales.

Whether offensive and defensive, in essence what these players are doing through performance is protecting their own opportunity that you are providing. But how do you measure their performance and effectiveness on your team? Great question! Get better at recognizing "dead weight." That's a real challenge with corporations, but it won't be for you. Corporations get so big that they end up with lots of dead weight and people who don't really have to produce a result in order to earn a paycheck. Like I said before, all they have to do is put their meat in a seat. They show up. That's all they have to do. You don't want this type of person on your team. You'd be doing a disservice to those members on your team who are good performers who produce results. Sometimes the challenge is that we don't know why we hired this person in the first place or how to get rid of them. But this is a whole other story that goes back to my argument about the defects in our educational system and a "tenure" mindset. If you have tenure, you don't have to perform. "I just exist and therefore I get more money." Unions… tenure… don't get me started! If you want to be on my team, you're going to have to produce value. Without producing value, we can't move forward as a team. We can't make great deals and bigger deals. I attract and only want to work with people who know that they can produce value either offensively or defensively.

If you don't know what value you can produce, it's probably because you have never produced value. In the defensive position there is operational efficiency. For example, you buy a vacant building. Before the defensive player was on board it took you six months to fill the building, but now with this person on board it takes you four months. While that may not seem like much to you, it means two months of occupancy that you didn't have before. Those two months of occupancy, depending on the size of the building, could be tens of thousands of dollars of additional revenue. I am almost willing to bet, depending on the size of the building again, the tens of thousands of dollars that this person helps to generate sooner is more than the salary that you are paying him/her all year. It should be! That's what I mean. If I could get all my buildings fuller just by two months, well, are you kidding? I'd be a happy, happy man!

I have a fabulous defensive player on my team. With her on board, we are saving more money than I dreamed possible in taxes through an agreement with the City of Memphis to provide certain benefits to our tenants in exchange for a freeze on our property taxes. That means no increase in property taxes! Am I excited about this? Am I happy to have the defensive player on my team that helped me find and implement this money-saving strategy? Uh, yes and yes!! On a portfolio the size of ours, that's about $150,000 a year

of savings on property taxes. That's $150,000 a year that will go back to the company in the form of profit but also be reinvested in the building in terms of capital expense.

As a business, especially an S Corporation like ours, you have more of a profit tax. You don't necessarily have an "income" tax and some people think that income and profit is the same thing. I assure you they are not. Understanding that difference is why some people pay more taxes than they have to and why others pay nothing. If you just understood what I said right there, well, excellent! Because, guess what? I am not going to explain it to you if you don't understand. As a real estate investor, it's something you truly need to understand and embrace. If you don't understand the difference between income and profit, I'm going to make you look it up and go on your own journey of discovery. Go figure it out! That's part of my purpose in writing this book. I'm giving you great information, but this is also an invitation... a push... for you to learn more and more about real estate investing. What do you draw from what you are reading today? How can it become a part of you? That is what it means to become educated. Don't stop here. Go to my site and read the books I recommend. They are excellent reads and you'll learn a lot! That's what I care about. I want you to learn from me, but also I want you to grow your curiosity and then learn from others. (Okay, now back to the regularly scheduled program... 'er, book!)

Why care about the difference between income and profit? Because you need to understand "capital expenditures" and how they affect your profit. I'm not going to talk about

capital expenditures and how to write those off and accelerate depreciation, but long story short, the government wants me to take a certain type of write-off in exchange for doing exactly what I do in providing clean, safe, affordable housing. Tenants want me to take the write off because now their building is even safer, more secure, cleaner, more fun, more something. The government is happy with us, the tenants are happy with us and, in theory, our occupancy goes up and our turnover goes down, which means we keep making more money, right? By providing clean, safe, affordable housing, and by working to get the tax write off, we just added another $100,000 or more of value in the building. Think about it. If it's ten buildings that are affected, that's another million dollars of value that my investors and I all get to share.

Could I have accomplished this alone? Heck, no. Alone I would have not had the time, skill or ability to actually complete the application, let alone take it through the process. Fortunately, I have a defensive player on staff who has the ability to do all of the steps and let's just say (and I'm making up numbers here) I pay that person $80,000 per year. If this one thing is all he or she did during the entire year, was it worth it? Uh, YES! That's what I am talking about when looking at team members. Of course, this one thing won't be all they do in a single year, but the point is that you have to hire people who are willing to produce those types of results for your company. The person in this scenario is my VP of Operations, and that's just one example of what she does to help my company and everyone involved in our deals.

I won't spend a lot of time talking about offensive players. We're moving into that now in a big way. We have marketing we've never had before, we're building the company's brand, and we're doing all sorts of new and exciting things. Like this book! That's new for me. It builds my brand. It serves to educate and expand my network. It can be a part of everything we do to raise awareness of our goals. We're even considering adding an affiliate strategy to our marketing. That's a terrific offensive move. Let's just say we have affiliates that are referring people to the website, to the membership program and all this other great stuff we're doing. That's an offensive move! No, we're not offending people. That's something I do regularly through my Carefrontation approach. (People tell me I have no filter. Hey, I'm working on it.)

Why is an affiliate program such a good offensive move? For one, affiliates are a variable expense. There is no "fixed" expense I have to pay. Affiliates decide they want to join in our effort and spread the message. The "variable" cost then is what percentage they earn from their efforts. It's a percentage of sales. Variable simply means I only incur the expense because a certain action happens. It is like commission. I don't incur commission unless they do or sell. I'm happy to pay variable expenses.

Create a good backup team, too.

When building your team you have to create a backup team. Why? Well, look at any sports team. Is there just one pitcher, one catcher, one coach or even one water boy? No. That would be a whole lot of pressure for that single individual. The same can be said of your team. Do not have a "single point of failure." You need to have people you can call on if something happens to your first string of defense. Add a first, second, third and even a fourth string! This is where your interpersonal skills and ability to build relationships come in.

What is a single point of failure? It can be a costly mistake. That's what! I know. If I had a backup property manager a couple of years back, I could have replaced my first-string property manager, which would have put a stop to his greedy ways. That was a lesson that cost me hundreds of thousands of dollars. Learn from my mistake. Don't have just one anything. Not just one property, of course, but also not just one professional on your team to handle different duties. Think in "strings."

I keep a backup list because I want to trust people 100%. If someone I trust ends up not being trustworthy, for example, a contractor or someone else involved in a distance deal, I move to the next such professional on the list. There is a hierarchy to our team so everyone plays a role in a deal. I understand hierarchy because I grew up in a military family. I developed a lot of my emotional intelligence there and then in life. I read a lot. I pray to stay centered, and I know how to keep my calm. I read this in David Sandler's sales books and I agree fully. He says, "If the leader loses his head, how can the team keep theirs?"

As the leader of the team, I would rather be respected than liked. I look for that in other people to add to my team. I look for good character first. Maybe he/she doesn't have the best skill set but great character. I can work with that! For example, a property manager who shows a lot of character and who does the job right is worth his/her weight in gold. This person is responsible for collecting rent, paying bills related to that property (or sending the bills on to the CFO), giving you reports and making sure the property is kept safe, sound and running well. How you find the right property managers is through, you guessed it, a series of questions. Ah, questions! I love questions. As you can see through this book, I truly believe that the answers are in the questions, and you can't be afraid to ask great questions. I'm not saying that you need to interrogate people, but you can ask a lot of questions during regular, non-stressful conversations. Here we are again… back at developing your interpersonal and communication skills!

Taking a property-management focus, I developed a list of questions that I've found really helpful to ask property managers. I include these in my RFPs (request for proposals) that I send to property managers. Let's say, for the sake of discussion, that you do all your numbers and that those numbers are based on your looking to buy and hold a property over the long haul. Your numbers are based on local market occupancy or vacancy rates. In this case, you want to ask your property management candidates:

1. "As the property manager for this property, you'd be in control of a lot of things. How would you propose

that we get this particular property to maintain an 85%, 95%, 105% or whatever the percentage occupancy rate that you want to maintain for your entire portfolio?" (This could be a single-family home you are thinking about adding to your portfolio of single-family homes that you rent out, or it could be multi-family dwellings or apartment complexes. The question is the same.)

2. "What is your strategy? What strategy would you employ to maintain this level of occupancy?" (You need to know the thinking of the property manager here, because your portfolio needs a certain level of occupancy to make it all work.)

3. "How long would it take for you to achieve that?" Or, "What would you need from me to make sure that you could do that?"

4. "When you've done that in the past, what was necessary, what pitfalls or what helped you to fall short that you don't want to have happen again to make sure that we could be successful?"

5. "What type of work do you prefer to do and what do you do best?" (This question is actually good for any member of the team you are thinking about bringing on.)

6. "Describe your company's process for collecting rents." (This is important because rent collection isn't always simple. Beyond proper accounting procedures, the property manager has to be able to manage other income-producing aspects of the property, like coin-operated washers and dryers. Or how about the management of the cell phone tower bill when you add

one of those to the property to make it more renter-friendly?)

7. "What is your process for retaining long-term tenants… tenants that last more than 12 months?" (Is the property management company known for complete tenant turnover? For example, on average, do tenants stay on their books five or six months and then leave suddenly? If so, there's probably a reason for that and you want to know that up front because that's going to affect your profitability. That's going to affect your bottom line, and it's your bottom line that you ultimately care about.)

8. "What is your company's maintenance policy and are you related to any of the vendors you are recommending?" (Sometimes this "happens." You'll find out too late if you don't ask that the property manager just happens to be related to the maintenance person who just happens to need some extra money, and suddenly guess what? When you need a wall painted in the building it doesn't get done. That's what happens!)

These questions are in addition to things you already know, like screening for quality tenants, eviction and collection procedures, and even advertising procedures. Like anything else in real estate and in life, the more questions you can ask, the better prepared you can be for any sort of emergency that can and will happen.

You have to ask these questions because you need to understand the strengths of the individuals you are considering for your team. For example, some property managers are great in managing higher-end properties, but they might prefer to manage lower-end properties. How will you learn this if you don't talk to them and ask questions? The alternative is hiring someone who would prefer to be managing lower-end properties when you've hired him/her to manage the higher-end properties. It doesn't make much sense. That person won't be happy; you won't be happy.

There are a few more questions I've learned to ask, such as what types if any political connections, city connections or inspector connections the property manager might have, and what else comes with these types of relationships? This is all about leveraging those relationships. I want to ask this question, because if the property manager ends up telling me that there is such a relationship in place, I might be able to leverage it and benefit from it in my business. Remember, I run a real estate investing business. Building my business is all about building relationships. If I know Suzy, who is now my property manager, and she knows a few people at City Hall, that might benefit me. There are times where you as the owner and landlord may need to call upon those additional individuals for assistance. It's a good idea to meet them ahead of time. That way, you put yourself out there and they know who you are already. Had I known to do that before the City of Memphis had passed the ordinance to penalize bad landlords, they would have known ahead of time that I'm not one of the bad guys. Quite the opposite. In fact, if you go on the offensive

here and practice a little preventative maintenance you could tell them you're there to help! That's what you need to do. Let them know early on.

Beyond the property manager...

Now, let's apply the questions to your construction contractor or clean-up crew or anyone on your team. You need to ask, for example, "What types of rehabs do you prefer to do? What type work and what type of materials do you prefer to work with?" The person's responses will give you what you need to know.

Let's say you're talking to a real estate professional. A great question to ask is, "If you had to choose an area of town to work in, which area would you choose and why?" The response will tell you a lot about the person's character and preferences, but it also serves to give you a lot of information about the marketplace. The answer will help you determine which parts of town to stay away from as an investor.

It's important to not just ask questions, but also to look at your vendors in a different light. They aren't just there to provide a service. Sure, you hire them to do different jobs, but guess what? They can help you expand your network, too. Why? Because the more people you know who have more and more skill sets, well, the more problems you as the real estate entrepreneur can solve. And it all starts with your building

a competent team. Hey, it's like ol' Benjamin Franklin said…
"An ounce of prevention is worth a pound of cure." Hiring on
character can save you a lot of hassle.

I wish I could train people for character. And integrity. But
this is hard to do. Character and integrity are part of a person.
These traits are built over time. I don't want to train people to
be better; I want to work with the best! It is very important to
work with character and integrity, no matter what line of work
you're in. But in real estate it is critical to have these traits.
Referrals will not happen if there is a seed of doubt about you
in the minds of the investors.

The truth about referrals.

People ask me about referrals. You might think they come
from all my leads. Well, some do, but that is not how I find
all my referrals. Some people find me. For example, I had one
man who paid me a lot of money to teach him what I know.
That was before I had moved into the education-provider
space. How did he find me? Through referral! Someone else
told him about what I did and have done. That was in 2011. It
was a pretty cool opportunity, and I thought it might help to
put me on my path as a real estate educator.

What lead to this fortunate opportunity was that I discovered
the Real Estate Radio Guys. I was so impressed by these
guys that I started going to their networking meetings. My
questions and answers were filled with more insight than a
lot of people in the room. That big-money referral was in the

room at one of the networking meetings. He approached me. The rest is history.

Why the Real Estate Radio Guys? At that time, I was looking for mentors. I didn't have anyone local. If I had a problem there was no one for me to turn to. My family couldn't help me. They didn't understand real estate investing. My wife and I no longer related to our peers. When I found the Real Estate Radio Guys I teamed up with them. They sponsor the cruises that Robert Kiyosaki and the Rich Dad organization go out on to teach financial intelligence (through the Cashflow game). They also sponsor other events in the industry. You can see how the chain of events went down. Popi and I now go on an annual cruise. At the time of this writing, I am now a part of the Summit faculty! I get to present onboard ship topics I love in real estate, and I get to lead a large Cashflow game. It's a honor to work with the Summit founders and other real estate investors. It's fun and exciting, too. Am I ever grateful to have found these Guys and their networking events. What if I'd been too afraid to put myself out there?

The other great thing here is that the Real Estate Radio Guys are working with me on projects. And now I can do some very fun projects internationally. Wonder why? Well, there is a really good quality of life in other places. Like Belize! It's beautiful there. The U.S. dollar goes really far in some countries. And if the news is accurate, we're facing a global economy meltdown. That means I need to be prepared. I need to establish a beachhead. So how do I go about that? I looked at places in the world where the U.S. dollar goes far. I looked at that and quality of life. Bingo! Belize.

In Belize, tourism is good. I believe a resort would do well there. So would a few other related businesses. Plus, I want to create jobs. The Belize worker is thrilled to receive 50 Belize dollars a day, which translates to $25 U.S. per day. And with that level of cost of living and wages (read: no tenure, unions, or other unproductive structures) I want a business in the service industry, and that's what we're doing. It will create income for me, the workers and the investors. My project in Belize sets families up for generations. We are solving a problem. It's easy to see the opportunity, so investors are happy to help.

Developing real estate in Belize is an appealing business and project because I now have the relationships to make it easy: land, laws, people, etc. In the U.S., all our rules make such a project costly and prohibitive. In the U.S., we have all sorts of insurance issues, labor laws, legal costs, we have to pay a lot higher wages and there are unions to work with. We also have Social Security to consider. All of these things made it prohibitive to choose the U.S. As an entrepreneur I see that these are obstacles and decided to look elsewhere to make my dream a reality. It is just easier in a foreign country. Besides, I get excited about how beautiful it is in Belize and by how nice the people are. It might make a good home one day for my wife and me. At least I have that option. The long and short of it is that I prevented a lot of headaches by choosing Belize as the location for the next big project to be involved in.

Speaking of prevention, you can prevent yourself a lot of headaches and heartaches, not to mention a hit to your wallet, by simply considering everything in a deal. This is where some investors really fall down. There is more to a deal than meets the eye, and it takes due diligence and a few phone calls to prevent any misunderstandings or surprise costs. There shouldn't be any surprises if you do your homework right, use your emotional intelligence and give the numbers a chance to tell you the truth. Your intent as a real estate investor isn't just to break even, right? Of course not! I give you things to consider when looking at properties next. I want you to make a profit, which means you have to look at everything in a deal... not just the sale price.

STEP SEVEN:

Don't Just Break Even…

Consider the Whole Package.

"Think left and think right and think low and think high. Oh, the thinks you can think up if only you try!" Dr. Seuss

People get really excited when participating in real estate. That's natural. It still happens to me. Every deal brings a new experience. That's what I like about investing in real estate. I keep learning and earning, learning and earning. New deals keep things fresh for me. But here is the downside to newbie investors. They get so caught up in finding and buying a piece of real estate for say a buy-and-hold strategy that they forget about the little or not-so-little things that tend to add up over time. For example, taxes and homeowner association dues that affect the amount of cash flow the investor will receive over time.

Taxes are overlooked more often than you might think. We

217

overlooked property taxes when we first started as investors, but not now. As I mentioned earlier, now we have frozen property taxes on some of our portfolio. But that's not because we're overlooking anything. Nope. It's because we were paying very close attention! The same holds true for every part of a deal and every expense, because every one of your expenses is someone else's income. That's right. Property taxes are income to the county. Property management fees are income to the property managers. Maintenance fees are income to the maintenance workers. When I put in cable to give tenants a better quality of life, guess what? That's income to the people who own the cable company. Or profits. Either way, it's money out of my pocket and into theirs.

Something people don't seem to know is that property taxes can be negotiated down. You have the right to try to reduce them. Property assessors have no apparent motivation to keep taxes high. They don't get a percentage of your tax dollars. They'll work with you if you approach them correctly. Use your best people skills!

Here's another little-known fact. Land is assessed improperly all the time, and the rules for reassessing usually allow you challenge the value. What does that mean to you, someone who might own a piece of land (on which your building sits)? You can have the land reassessed and save yourself tax dollars. "But what about comps, J.?" Don't worry about comps. They are based on old values. When you get to my team's level of investing, easily you can spend six figures a year on property taxes. You should manage those property taxes. It's not as

hard as it sounds. In fact, it's a simple process that takes time. You can handle it yourself or hire a CPA at a percentage of what you pay in taxes. However, you can choose to let your property taxes go unaddressed. But if you let them get out of control they will stay out of control!

As you can see, owning a property isn't automatically an asset. This is absolutely true until it becomes profitable. Passive income doesn't mean you don't have involvement. Quite the opposite! I have systems in place so that I don't have to be involved in every aspect of the deal. I walked you through that in the teamwork section. You know how I know that I have the right team in place? They produce more value than the wage they receive!

What about those maintenance fees?

Truth: you're gonna incur maintenance fees. Even if you don't buy property in a community that requires you to pay road maintenance fees or land maintenance fees, you will still incur maintenance fees in other forms. For instance, what if the roof springs a leak after a big rain? It takes money and/or time to repair that part of the roof, doesn't it? Call it a maintenance fee. Maybe a kid down the street lobs a ball through a window of your newly purchased piece of real estate. Guess what? Cha-ching. It takes money to fix the window. For the sake of this conversation, let's call it a maintenance fee.

If you are investing in property to fix 'n' flip, there will be plenty of upfront costs. You can lose money in a fix 'n' flip, too. And when you go to sell it, you will make a profit - maybe. And if you do, guess what? That's possibly ordinary income or a capital gains tax you just inherited, as well. Now, it's what you do with that profit that matters. And with certain more elaborate business structures you have a certain time frame to flip it into another property. That's one reason you'll be doing more and more, and bigger and bigger deals! Unless you want to pay taxes on the profit.

Whether you are rehabbing a property or fixing it up to flip it, you will incur costs. Even keeping repairs down to a bare minimum and doing the smaller jobs yourself will cost you money. Paint costs money. Nails cost money. Wood and shingles cost money. Well, you get my drift. I was once really interested in fixing and flipping, but I soon learned that is not where my passion lies. You won't be surprised that I feel this way when I share with you my tale of Fix 'n' Flip Gone Wrong! (I told you I'd get to this story.)

I'm actually going to tell you about more than just the fix 'n' flop. I'll share with you about one of the biggest mistakes I ever made. This was in 2009… yep, not that long ago. The mistake was allowed to happen because I perceived myself as the weaker partner, and I gave up control to make decisions. (As in I didn't make the decisions; my partners did.) The smart thing I did – though I did not plan it – is that I handled the mail. The mail came to me and I could see the paper trail of the money being spent. Here is where

my emotional intelligence showed through. My emotional intelligence was better than my partners' emotional intelligence. We were fixing and flipping together, and I was on the hook for $100,000. I had given over my control and had no way to get it back. Things went from bad to worse. First my contractor had a nervous breakdown followed by a divorce. Then someone stole my floor. Yes, my entire floor... all the flooring! Then we learned that the titles were clouded. And the guy who sold us the property went to jail for FTC fraud. The FBI placed him in the slammer!

What did I do next? A lot of soul-searching. There's one thing I absolutely did not do, however. I did not hide from my investors' phone calls. I was honest. As a result one of the investors said he'd give me more money. I was floored and asked him why. "You are a safer bet because you will never do that again." So, you see, mistakes have value. Integrity has value. I'm still paying some of those investors back on this fix 'n' flop; many have already recouped their monies. It was not their fault that things went wrong. One of the lessons I learned is that there is a seed of something great in every mistake we make. You have to face your mistakes and then move through them. Find the silver lining.

Another mistake I made was having a single point of failure. I was working with the same contractor and the same property management company on different deals. Now I know not to have just one point of contact. I learned through trial and error. Through mistakes! For example, in one of our apartment complexes, the rent roll showed that the rents of some of the units were being paid. The same guy who was responsible for collecting rents also was responsible for paying the utilities. This was a mistake, because it could be a huge "profit" for him when he didn't actually pay the utilities. Our CFO said something seemed off. It made us look closer. We learned that the guy was skimming money!

We had to extricate this person. We had a problem. I was afraid of what would happen. We had a single point of contact, which was frightening for me to look at. This was also right before I was in a very bad car accident. I wasn't sleeping. I was not in the right frame of mind to make decisions. The idea of firing the person was absolutely painful. It was like receiving perpetual bad news. We had to get the guy out, change our systems, create dual points of contact, create new cash-control systems and a new rehab process, etc. However, we couldn't do anything with the property until we had gotten everything worked out. Before we could get through all of that, the mayor of Memphis held a press conference located on our property! He announced that he was suing all the "negligent" property owners who are doing nothing with properties. We were named in the lawsuit! But that's not all we had to deal with.

Months later we got a call about one of our newly rehabbed properties. We were moving people in at that point. The call? My building was on fire! Fourteen units had burned and we had 16 units left. The public insurance adjuster and every investor needed to know. I had never dealt with something like this. My team and I had a conference call to see if all the members would stay on with me. "Are you in or are you out?"

That's what I asked each of them. None left; they are still with me today. About that time I was learning how property insurance actually worked. (You may think you know, but you don't until you have a potential multi-million dollar claim.) While dealing with my fears, while dealing with my burned building and the lawsuit (about being a "negligent" property owner), I found out my rental property where my wife and I lived had developed a big problem… mold. I have asthma, so that means I could die from the mold. Then I got another call. My apartment building had burned again. This time the city tore it down without informing me. So now our first fire insurance claim was in danger.

This might have stopped me from being a real estate investor had I not had a strong team. I didn't have to deal with things alone. We dealt with everything together. We found out the other property with that "evil" manager had been doing the same thing to other owners. He did about $800,000 in damage overall. We were pursuing him legally and had a judgment against him. We got another call. The guy had been shot seven times point blank. Apparently one of the other real estate owners wasn't as patient and understanding as we were.

My fears stopped me from making faster decisions. My team was looking to me to direct them. So I learned to be a better leader. Now things are great. The team and I stuck through all the hard events with the apartment rehab and the fix 'n' flop. We are doing much better and we're vastly better than we've ever been! We learned from our mistakes. We had to get our systems operating better. No investor lost a payment.

However, we did have to renegotiate with a couple of them. Overall, they were pretty understanding.

The problems we encountered with the fix 'n' flop and the rehab made us a stronger team. Now I know the team is here by choice, because they stayed. Some people ask how did I get through all of this? I had to find the motivation within myself. To be honest, I stayed up all night and prayed Isaiah 43, which loosely discusses having a companion even during times of my greatest fear. God will not give me, or you, more than we can bear. And now when I have fears of any sudden disaster; I know I can live through them. When I worry about tomorrow I have tangible evidence in my own life of how to overcome.

With all the mistakes and the problems we went through, I developed a new talent of dealing with difficult situations. I had to keep my faith and develop courage. I know that bad things might happen in the future, but I know we can get on the other side of it. The real question becomes when are we out of the woods? I've come to realize that risk in inherent in living and the woods never really end until you expire. With that new outlook, we now have the systems, courage, and ability to work internationally to develop large apartment complexes and commercial buildings. I may have more than a few battle scars, and you may look down on me and tell me how you would have never done it like that, and ask how could I be so ignorant, etc., but that's real estate investing. It's like the Wild, Wild West! It's not like missing a coffee break. You better strap yourself into the saddle and get ready for a

rough ride some days. Like Theodore Roosevelt said, "Get ready to enter the ring."

Environment trumps will.

I could be someone different had my mother not married a military man. For example, after my deal went horribly wrong, I had paralyzing fear and couldn't make a decision, but I moved through it. My balanced, disciplined upbringing allowed me to see that the mayor was just doing his job. I couldn't blame anyone for the events. They happened and I'd have to deal with the outcome. Unfortunate timing for us, I guess. And things worked out in the end even better than I could have imagined. The mayor and I are now on more amicable speaking terms. The City of Memphis now understands who we are and that we had not changed to be in compliance with the lawsuit, but that we were always that way. Now the intent will be to help out with other buildings. New relationships were forged. We now have a new and better system. The point is that at the end of the day there is an action component to everything we do. And all of that comes from be willing to make a mistake, or two, or three, or four...

Not to keep bashing our education system, but another thing that is wrong with it is that we are not taught to take action. We are taught to wait for a teacher to tell us what to do. "Hey," we think, "there is no homework! There must be nothing more to do." But this needs to change. Ask questions. Act on your answers. Act at the speed of instruction. Don't wait until you get home. Here is an example. If I'm at a seminar and I learn

225

something new and we have a 15-minute break, I will apply what I just learned. By doing so I have leapfrogged because I collapsed the time to make my progress faster. I assimilate faster by putting whatever I learn by doing fast. Fail fast. Learn. Move on. I have had fantastic failures. If you want to hear about them, listen to my podcast on fantastic failures.

The point is that even after what could be considered fantastic failure events, I didn't quit. Please don't read that last line thinking that I wasn't tempted to quit or that I didn't contemplate quitting. If you do this business or any business and aren't tempted to quit then you're likely not committed in the first place. Now, promise me that you won't quit once you encounter difficult situations in real estate. Create your vision and take the steps to make it happen. Life can change with a phone call! So make a lot of phone calls. Alone I am not strong enough to do what needs to be done. I call on my team and on God. I suggest the same for you. My job is to guide the ship, because it must be guided by some sound principles. Then professional education is important. It doesn't have to be YOUR professional education, however. For example, I don't need to know the difference between contract law and employee law. And I don't have to know how to fill out the contract. The person who is hired to create the contract needs to know. I may not be the best CEO yet, but the exciting part is that I keep learning so I will be one day. And you get to come along on my journey! You get to watch my progress. Talk about accountability! Whew…

You know one of the things I have learned in this role as team leader (a.k.a., CEO)? It's that thinking outside the box is an absolute necessity for my team's success!

STEP EIGHT

Think Outside the Box!

"I saw an angel in the marble and carved until I set him free."
Michelangelo

In the beginning of my real estate investing journey, my credit score was really low (398 to be exact). I had no credit. I couldn't go to the bank and ask for a loan. Think about this... What if you go to the bank with that kind of score and no credit and then you ask for a loan to invest in real estate? What do you think the answer would be? Of course it's a big NO WAY. If you're in that boat, like me, you'd be forced to think around that wall and outside the box. In this case the "box" is a house or "real estate." You have to think a lot differently than you do as a homeowner, too. You're going to have to figure out who you are as an investor, and then whom you are serving.

Once you understand your investor identity and the different identities the investors you are seeking, you can then target

229

those markets. Next you assemble a team and share your vision with everyone you know. If everyone understands your identity and your target (your demographic), they'll help you hit that target dead center. Remember… you don't put the Wal-Mart greeter at the front of Nordstrom. It won't work very well.

Targeting your demographics takes skills.

Start with who you are as a person and work outward. Learn to serve your culture first. I don't mean necessarily your ethnicity, but rather your buying habits, living habits, work habits, etc. That is your culture. Take a good look at your habits, your likes and your dislikes. Based on what you learn about yourself, you will make choices in how you rehab a building that would appeal to someone in your culture right down to the materials you use.

It is value that determines the materials that you use in any project. Think of it this way. It's the dollar movie experience versus the hundred-dollar luxury theater experience. You won't find that those two theaters are the same. If you want to best serve the people who attend the dollar theater you will be buying different components to rehab the property than if you're serving the higher-dollar-value customer. To determine what base you are serving, take a look around at the geography. Look at the retail spaces in a geographic area. Are there pawnshops? Are there 7/11s or Starbucks? If there are pawnshops, that means housing is functional and affordable,

but it also has to be appealing in appearance. You must understand your customer. You have to understand where you come from first and then you understand what other people want. What is the experience of the people you want to serve?

Invest in WHERE you know.

People tell me that I cannot or should not invest outside of my own state. You might've heard these people say for you to stay in your own backyard. But what if that backyard happens to be so expensive that you can't really effectively invest in real estate to make a good profit? That's the case in California, Hawaii, and New York. I happen to live in southern California, and it's pretty expensive here. I have an affinity for Memphis, where real estate is much more affordable. So that's where I invest a lot.

But how do you buy property in another state if you're not there physically to make the decision? We covered this in an earlier step, but to refresh your memory, my advice is to choose a place you actually know. Maybe you know Texas. Maybe you know people in Texas who could actually look at properties for you. I do this from time to time, or at least I did when I was first starting my real estate career. I like to share a story at my workshops about that. I was just learning about investing and the instructor said something about property in another state. I immediately looked one up that happened to be located not far from where my brothers and my mother live. I asked them to go look at it for me. Long story short, I didn't get that property, but I proved to myself that I could have other people I trust look at property in other states. That experience was for ... well, experience! I'd be making plenty of deals and profit soon enough.

If you don't have eyes in other states, you certainly have Internet access. Like I said earlier, you can start looking at properties with Google Earth maps. If you can go to the area, that's excellent. You can look for certain demographic clues. For example, are there senior centers in the area? That would be a clue to what type of home buyer and seller you would find. It's a clue to the type of homes that you will find in that area that dictates costs and such.

There are certain demographic shifts that have occurred in the family structure in our country. Everything, for example, has shifted to a two-child home-building model. This is a trend, and I look at everything through the goggles of real estate. Everything is real estate. I cannot help but look at everything in an area and translate that in my mind to being real estate. I look at everything, even trash cans. Are they open and available to everyone or are they hidden behind something? Is there central air or window units? Are most of the buildings one-story or are there three floors and no elevator? This tells you something. If it's a three-floor building with no elevator it may not be a good deal because you will have trouble filling that third floor with tenants. You may wonder how I came up with the idea of gathering demographic information without paying for market research. I sort of owe that to my mother!

Rather, I owe it to a visit from my mother who needed hair products. (She wanted to look fabulous for my wedding.)

As you know, I live in Orange County, California. My mother lives in North Carolina. When she was here in the OC for my wedding she wanted to buy some hair products, so a friend, my best man at the wedding, took her to a drugstore. In North Carolina where my mom lives, the population mix is different than it is in Orange County. As a result, my mom couldn't find any of her hair care products. Ta-da! It dawned on me that this is a great way to look at an area I'm considering in real estate. I can learn everything I need to know by visiting local stores! Say you drop me somewhere, anywhere in the country, and I want to know the demographics of the area. One of the first things I am going to do is to make a trip to the local brand-name drugstore and make a beeline to the hair care aisle. What I see in that store will tell me a lot about who is in that neighborhood. I can begin to get my bearings about the customer, which tells me what type of real estate could do well in the area (because I know who I am serving). If I don't know who I am serving I can't make the real estate do what it needs to do. I know this seems like a little thing, but I am just saying the clue is there: Target or Walgreens? Wal-Mart or Nordstrom?

All these stores have way more money to do demographics studies than I do, and they are only going to carry products that sell. The only products that are going to sell are the ones that customers need. Look at McDonalds. There's a McDonalds almost anywhere you travel, but the one in Maine sells lobster. The one in southern California doesn't. Lobster sells well in Maine. In Hawaii it's something different. In Louisiana, it's something different yet again! McDonalds caters to the customer. I am not a genius. This is real basic stuff here, and if it is good for Walgreen's it works for me. If a drugstore doesn't have Black hair care products that's because not many Black folk are living in the area.

Try this... Next time you find a Nordstrom department store, see if there's an Apple store nearby. I am almost willing to bet the Apple store is in close proximity, because the two stores go together. They serve the same customer type. Seeing these two stores tells you the demographics of that area. You don't see one without the other, and they are in that same area because there is a certain customer that Nordstrom and/or Apple are looking to attract. When you recognize those trends you know what area of town you're in. This helps me a lot when I am traveling. I'll ask someone, "Where is your Nordstrom (or other high-end department store) located?" When I get my answer, it tells me about the real estate around the area. Where there is an upscale department store, I know the people in the area probably have white-collar jobs. White-collar real estate is different; or rather apartment buildings run differently in those areas. I'm looking for the lower-income stuff.

In a lower-income area, you won't see a Nordstrom or Apple store. You won't see large chain grocery stores either. You'll see convenience stores and liquor stores. That's where the people go to get their groceries. I know the rules in these areas; it is just different rules for different areas. That's where my

whole Wal-Mart, Target and Nordstrom strategy comes from...
through simple observation. All three of these companies
currently have more money than I do, they have more people
whom they pay who have more degrees than I have or want,
and they do all the research for me. This is just one way that I
identify the opportunity. After all, real estate is about trends,
right? It is about slow-moving trends. In this case, what I also
want to know is where the Nordstrom is going to be built.
That's easy enough. I type in NORDSTROM COMING SOON
in my search bar and Google it. Then I need to figure out
where the city is trying to allocate funds next.

I can find out where the city is planning to allocate funds.
This isn't brain surgery. There is usually an association of
governments for every county, so you enter a county name
or association of governments into your search bar and hit
ENTER. These sites will tell you all about the city's ten-year
plan and what they intend to do with all of that tax money
that is coming in. Cool. Thank you. I can use this information
to my benefit. It is a road map to future great areas in that
city. Pay attention to the newspaper, too, especially during
election time. These guys are making promises right and left
that hopefully they can fill about creating better communities,
cleaning up dilapidated areas, putting money into a city to
make it nicer. Some will; some won't. The point is to look at
their plans.

Another thing I do is set up alerts online that send me this
type of information because it can become daunting trying to
keep track of it all. But there are programs out there where you

can request, "Send me all news articles that say real estate in Memphis." If Memphis is mentioned someplace in an article I receive that article in my email box. Do that for Apple stores and Nordstrom or whatever you're interested in learning about. It's a simple thing to do, but not a lot of people know to do it. Hey, it's my gift to you!

Building type matters, too.

My building selection is based on demographics. For example serious college students may like rectangular buildings. Rectangular shaped buildings may not be good. I search for U-shaped buildings that promote more community among the residents. Single people who are also professionals who don't have a lot of time to socialize may be found in a rectangular apartment building. For families, buildings with the courtyard are good. Also a U-shaped building with the courtyard or swimming pool in the middle can be good for singles that want to mingle. Multi-family dwellings that cater to culinary students means we can add a communal kitchen. If there is space for a day care center in a family-centric apartment building we can add one for families as a value-added bonus.

Most of my buildings are on a bus route. Even if the building comes to me at a great discount, but it's not a bus route, I might pass. I want the building on a bus route, especially since a lot of my tenants don't have cars. Again you have to understand your customer. You have to understand the smallest nuances. For example, say the basketball team in a certain neighborhood is winning and you notice that rent is

paid on time more often than when the team isn't winning. You need to know that kind of stuff. Invest your time in understanding your customer. Ask yourself, "Do I want my tenant to be the same person who shops at Nordstrom?" If so, your doorknob is going to be different than for the tenant who shops at Target.

If you don't know an area, it is a really good idea to make inroads with good Realtors and good real estate companies. For example, online there is a real estate-related website called Active Rain and there's also Realtor.com, and you can always search on Facebook, LinkedIn, or NARPM.org for good property managers. Property managers certainly know the area they serve. These professionals will help you by telling you about the type of person who would live there. They would know what would be of interest to a certain type of customer, for example, land, older architecture, even what type of foods they like. In Maine they like lobster. I know that sounds like a given, but what type of lobster, how often do they eat it and where do they go to eat it, what type of restaurants? A property manager or a good Realtor in that area would actually be able to answer those questions. They would also know what type of retail establishments are in the area. In Maine there a lot of mom-and-pop operations. That means homemade products vs. department stores.

When looking at real estate, for example, when I'm looking for certain apartment buildings in different areas, I want to know their proximity to schools and hospitals. I want to know if it's walking distance from shopping centers and parks. I want to know as much as I can. If something is missing, like a good laundry room, we can add one. It becomes a bonus for the residents. Something like this would make it ultimately more attractive for potential renters.

Is the area pet-friendly? I need to know that so I can choose the right type of flooring. I wouldn't want to have carpet in an apartment that's very pet-friendly. Maybe I could make it a pet-only building. In that case, instead of a pool I would consider a dog run. All of these questions come from understanding your customer. That's why I dig real estate! I get to ask a lot of questions. You must make it a place to live, play and lay for others to be interested in renting the space you are creating. If you buy an old, decrepit building, and then you make enhancements during the rehab process, you better understand your customer. If not you're going to have a lot of empty apartments.

Maybe you want to cater to lawyers in Washington, D.C. You better understand the size of the entryway, the importance of a good coat closet and other amenities that other buyers/renters don't necessarily care about. In Washington, D.C, residents tend to throw a lot of impressive fundraisers. Their living space, therefore, must allow for such activities. Again, it's all about understanding the customer.

Comps are irrelevant.

People ask me about comps in relation to real estate investing.

Comps are irrelevant in investing. I don't care about comps. The house is worth what I am willing to pay for it. Comps may matter when you as a homebuyer go to a real estate agent. In that case, the agent will show you comps (comparative properties that have sold) based on what the neighbors' homes are worth. This is not the same thing. When I look for buildings or property, I'm looking at how I can improve them and raise the value either to rent it out or to sell it. Values are assigned. There is a use value. And that's really the highest value that is assigned. You will pay most for the use value. There is also speculation, for example, where you would pay the least. Investment falls somewhere in the middle. You have to look at the use value and the speculative value to figure out what you might offer. That said, you can start your negotiations at a buck. (Making an offer is only an invitation to start a conversation.)

Seriously, there is no rule that says you cannot start your negotiations at one dollar. No, you likely won't get the property, but it certainly opened a conversation, didn't it? You may think I'm joking, but I've done this. I've offered a ridiculously low amount for a property. It obviously works. I have hundreds of units to prove it.

You have to look for pain points. For example, I bought a 18-unit complex from a guy who had bought the wrong type building for him because he didn't know how to serve the customer. In that complex a couple of the units were just one-bedrooms. I turned one of them into a laundry room. Why? I was solving a problem. I was answering a pain point. There was no laundry room. The tenants needed one.

In rehabbing, we look at things that are going to reduce our costs in the long run, too. For example, I like to put in low-flow toilets because water costs money. How can I save money on water costs? Ah... low-flow toilets!

A good thing to do is ask a property manager about properties in his/her area that have problems. I love problems! I am the problem solver. That's what you want to be, too. As a problem solver you can make a very good income in real estate. Let's just run some numbers, shall we? Let's say that you know when you buy a property, a multi-family dwelling in this case, that has eight units, and each unit can bring a rent of $450 a month. Multiplying the $450 by the eight units equates to $3,600 per month. That's a good gross revenue. In a short time, you'll have money to invest in your next property. Or maybe you're going to do the fast track like I did, using other people's money and credit to buy properties, and you're able to move on quickly to the next deal. In the next deal, there is a 10-unit dwelling that you know can rent for $425 per unit. Quickly calculating, that is $4,250 per month. Add that to you $3,600 a month and what do you have?

Let's just say, for the sake of argument, you moved quickly like I have told you to do. Over a year's time you have purchased one 8-unit complex, a 10-unit complex, two 12-unit complexes, a 16-unit complex, a 17-unit complex, a 29-unit complex, a 30-unit complex and a 34-unit complex. Then you were fortunate

to find a 182-unit complex. You can do the math on that or I can save you from the math right now. That is a total potential of $166,825 per month. That equates to more than $2 million annually. So… are you interested in becoming a real estate investor now?

Avoiding and preparing for RISK. (No, not the board game.)

You have to mitigate risk. There are things that you will never be able to know because you really aren't a Securities and Exchange Commission (SEC) professional. That's why it's good to have an SEC professional you can go to with your questions and to help you research issues. For example, in the Jobs Act the SEC says that you and I can place ads to raise private capital now. But you still have to stick to their limitations. Talk to a securities attorney and find out the rules before you place any ads. For example, there are different rules for an accredited investor. But what does that mean? You have to learn what it means and then you have to look for information, so you won't be doing anything illegal.

I happen to know what an "accredited investor" means. If you're single it means you have made $200,000 in the prior two years. If you're married, it's $300,000. Or you have a net worth of $1M in exclusion of your primary residence. Even as an accredited investor you have to follow the SEC rules. Perhaps the fastest track to reading these rules is to go to SEC. gov. As of July 10, 2013, the rules changed. However, I am not going to tell you about what those rules are. You will have to first read about them and then contact an SEC attorney. I do know that one of the rules is around crowd funding. And the topic of crowd funding is going to be something you will want to research, as many will be riding this wave to financial freedom.

The Reg. D Exemption and other wonders...

The Regulation D Exemption is pretty exciting for you as an investor and you need to learn more about how this regulation affects you. Here is something I lifted from the U.S. Securities and Exchange Commission's website that will help you understand:

Rule 506 of Regulation D is considered a "safe harbor" for the private offering exemption of Section 4(2) of the Securities Act. Companies using the Rule 506 exemption can raise an unlimited amount of money. A company can be assured it is within the Section 4(2) exemption by satisfying the following standards:

• The company cannot use general solicitation or advertising to market the securities;

• The company may sell its securities to an unlimited number of "accredited investors" and up to 35 other purchases. Unlike Rule 505, all non-accredited investors, either alone or with a purchaser representative, must be sophisticated—that is, they must have sufficient knowledge

and experience in financial and business matters to make them capable of evaluating the merits and risks of the prospective investment;

• Companies must decide what information to give to accredited investors, so long as it does not violate the antifraud prohibitions of the federal securities laws. But companies must give non-accredited investors disclosure documents that are generally the same as those used in registered offerings. If a company provides information to accredited investors, it must make this information available to non-accredited investors as well;

• The company must be available to answer questions by prospective purchasers;

• Financial statement requirements are the same as for Rule 505; and

• Purchasers receive "restricted" securities, meaning that the securities cannot be sold for at least a year without registering them.

But what does that mean for real estate investors like you? It could mean that if you follow certain rules that you can raise "unlimited cash." However, your SEC attorney can help you figure this part out. Again, there are rules. You need to educate yourself.

There's also something that you need to understand about the Patriot Act. I won't go into it here and this is something you need to speak to your attorney about, but it involves how currency moves. There must be a verifiable paper trail on currency amounts more than $9,999.99 when this money is transferred into the U.S. from another country, or anywhere really. However, some foreign investors understand this rule and they are prepared when you begin working with them. And before you go international, become a successful real estate investor on the home front. Invest in your country first. Market locally.

Pushing your message locally.

The way I pushed my message out is through advertising, for example postcards on cars, public speaking, radio and TV. But one of the best ways to tell people about what I do and to get them involved is by playing the Cashflow 101 board game. This game attracts the person who is looking to be involved in investing in real estate. At the end of the game I simply ask, "Would you like to do what you did in the game in real life?" The answer is always yes. If the answer is yes and I really believe they're serious about it, I ask the person to meet me at Starbucks, we agree on a time and then we talk.

When I am in a face-to-face situation and I'm talking to people who seem to be interested in getting involved in real estate investing I have a script that I stick to. I do not waver from this script because it works. When you are talking to people

about real estate investing… after you understand what you're doing… you can use the same script and you will not waver. It goes exactly like this:

Me: "Have you ever considered getting involved in real estate investing?"

It doesn't matter the response of the listener. No matter what he or she says, my response will remain the same. I will say, "Really? Why?"

Here it is very important for you to listen to what that person has to say. They'll tell you why they're interested in real estate investing, for instance, because their relatives have done really well in the real estate market. They'll tell you all sorts of reasons they want to get involved and all sorts of reasons why they don't want to be involved. They will tell you the horror stories they've heard about other people who have been involved in real estate investing and haven't done well. You are not here to convince them to get into real estate. You were only listening at this point so that you can gather information and solve their problems. That's what you want to be. Remember… you want to be a problem solver. That requires listening skills.

If the person tells you that they are interested in becoming a real estate investor, but they say something like, "Yes, I have considered this, but I don't like tenants," because you are listening, you just heard their pain point. And the answer is that they don't want to have to deal with tenants. They can still be a real estate investor and not deal with tenants. You will deal with tenants.

If they say yes but they don't have time or yes but they only have a little bit of money, you can work with that. Here it is very important that you understand the 70/30 Rule in which you are listening for 70% of the time and asking questions, very simple questions, the other 30% of the time. You are trying to learn everything you possibly can to help that person become the real estate investor that they really want to be. Creating wealth is a team sport and you are always recruiting. This is not just to benefit your bank account. It is to benefit everyone involved.

If they say yes, and then they ask is $XXX enough, you always say, "That's a start!" That's because they always have more than they are disclosing. Rarely will a person fully disclose exactly how much money they have to invest. They will... in time. First trust must be built. This trust will happen because you will be honest. You will earn the trust; you do not own the trust. For the record, earning one's trust requires great listening skills.

When you're listening to people, you have to be vastly aware of cultural mindsets and practices around money and investing. Different cultures handle money and investing differently. I will not go into stereotypes here, but I will say sometimes stereotypes are there for a reason. Some cultures have a matriarchal structure and some cultures have a patriarchal structure. Some cultures believe in keeping

money in the family, whereas here in America we are raised with a very eco-centric viewpoint in which we are very individualized in our money and investing practices. It would benefit you to learn how different cultures handle money and think about money and investing before talking to them. In the beginning, stick to the audience you know. That will be people who share your same value structure around money and investing. There is less of a learning curve that way.

When you're talking to people about becoming real estate investors and doing a deal with them, you are not just interviewing to find pain points and problems you can solve. You are also interviewing for character type, emotional intelligence, mindset and that person's financial situation. By understanding the person and his viewpoints you can keep yourself from taking money from the wrong people. You might wonder how I know this. It might just be that I took money from the wrong people and it made a couple of my deals more difficult than they should have been. I know better now. Interviewing for character, emotional intelligence and learning all I can about the person's viewpoints around money helps me to not make this mistake again.

Be a PIG!

No… I am not telling you to go home and make a mess of things. That will just frustrate your significant other. I am telling you to become a professional information gatherer (PIG). When you're talking to people about investing, you have to understand them. You have to meet them "where

they're at." But that's not all. You also have to get the details
on what they might be earning on their investments right now.
You have to get a full picture of their financials in just a few
responses. You have to be a very good listener. For example,
maybe they have their money stuffed in a CD in the bank.
You can ask them, "So you're getting about 1% now on your
savings in the bank?"

If the response is a big and disappointed YES, you can offer
them a higher return than 1% on their money. If you can offer
them more, don't you think they might want to put their
money into your real estate investment deal? The chances are
high once they understand the rules. For example, maybe you
can give them as much as a 5% return on their money over
time. That's five times what they're earning currently with
their CD! Once they understand how you will use their money
and give them back their investment plus more over time
(because you've told them "this is what my company does...")
it will make more sense to them to come on board with you
as an investor. You are actually solving a problem for them
that they didn't know they had. They wanted more return on
their money than they have in the bank. Investing in your real
estate deal, they can get that. This is not to say that you have
to give them 5%, because you would want to work your way
up to that. (Negotiate up to that if you have to, but otherwise
offer more than they are currently earning in interest and less
than you actually can offer. This gives you plenty of wiggle
room in your negotiations.) Why would you offer 5% when
they would possibly agree to 4%? After all, that is more than
they are getting in their CD, right?

Some people think that it takes only one or two investors to fund the deal. That could be true, but I can take a lot of different investors and put their money to good use in different projects. Hard costs have to be covered. For example, the most obvious hard cost is the down payment or full purchase price. Then there are the renovation costs. I make sure that everything works well, because I have a team behind me. Each member of that team has a job so that things run like clockwork when it comes to contracts, to escrow and to making monthly payments to investors.

When I am renovating a building that I have purchased, for example an apartment building, I want to make sure that the rent I am offering is lower than the rents of the surrounding buildings. I do this strategically to push people to move to my building. Ideally if the other buildings go vacant, I can buy those buildings and renovate them. It just makes good business sense. Take a look at some of my renovations on these next pages.

Before

After

Before

After

Before

After

These renovations took a lot of work, but it was well worth it. Now I can provide clean, safe, affordable housing to a lot of families! Notice that I didn't say "these took a lot of money" because that shouldn't be your focus if you're doing rehabs. Let me explain.

With each renovation my team and I have to think outside "the box" to come up with creative solutions for getting the work done as quickly and affordably as we can. We don't just utilize OPM to get things done. We also rely on OPK (other people's knowledge) and OPT (other people's time). This is not brain surgery. It's smart, and you will have to embrace the concept of using OPE (other people's everything). Different people bring different skills and abilities. I rank OPK at the top of my list. As I've mentioned, I don't have to know how to do everything if other people are competent in skills I don't happen to possess. And if these people also have TIME to devote to projects that I don't, even better. I can leverage that, too! It's all about thinking creatively, which is what we talk about in the next step.

STEP NINE

Think Creatively

"Imagination will often carry us to worlds that never were. But without it we go nowhere." Carl Sagan

You might wonder why I titled this section of the book "Think Creatively" when the last section was titled "Think Outside the Box." They may sound like the same thing, but I assure you they are not. In the last section I guided you to think about "the box," which is "the house" or piece of real estate you want to buy and then think beyond that box to other types of real estate to consider when investing. In this step I'll show you how to look at your investment creatively to discover new ways of making more cash *flow* into your hands. I'm going to give you bit more of a glimpse into the way I think, too.

Say you have found a few pieces of real estate that you think make good investments. Now let's say that one of the pieces is a multi-family housing unit with four living spaces. It needs work, so you aren't sure about investing. How would you turn this problem into a good investment? How would you go about creating the most cash flow with this piece of real estate? You will have to put on your thinking cap and be creative. Don't just see this piece of real estate as a problem. Take it beyond the numbers! Go as far as you can in your vision and then push yourself to see further. This is not elementary school where our penchant for thinking creatively is flattened under the feet of well-meaning teachers. Quite the contrary. I want you to think as creatively about this piece of property as you can. Think first about what it would take to bring this property up to snuff to a point that families and individuals would want to live there. Does it have broken windows? Is the wood rotted and in need of replacing? What does the overall exterior structure look like? What about the interior? What about the laundry area? What's that like? Make a list.

List in hand; start thinking who you could hire to do repairs. Can YOU do any of them and, if so, is that work going to add or take away from your life? Do you have enough time to devote and are your skills enough that your repairs will pass muster with the city? It might surprise you, but I don't want you to do everything yourself. You might think that by doing repairs yourself you can save money. To a certain degree you could be right, but isn't it better to hire someone for a fair wage who can do the work so you can get on with all the other things on your plate? For example, maybe you have other properties that need your investment. I remind you that I said you need to move quickly and do more deals faster. If you

stop to make all the repairs on pieces of real estate that you invest in, how will you find time to go get your next deal?

Where can you find good sources of labor? My next suggestion might jolt you a little, but have you ever thought about giving ex-convicts a chance? What about those individuals who are seeking Visas to stay in the United States? Perhaps you would consider hiring troubled youth. Not only would you be helping these pools of individuals by giving them an opportunity to prove themselves as good workers, but some states actually give rebates for using state-involved (nice way to say ex-con) individuals and youth that need some extra attention so they don't become convicts. Get in touch with your city, county and state legislation to learn what labor pools might be open to you. You might save money and save lives at the same time.

You might worry about the security of your property if you hire from these labor pools. However, you need to stop that line of thought. Hiring them will actually solidify the security of your building because these individuals need a second chance. They are grateful for that chance. They know when someone is up to no good and can alert you if they see suspicious activity. (They'll spot it before you do. You might not even recognize the activity as being suspicious!) They'll feel good about helping you, and you can feel good knowing you're helping them create a different type of life. It's almost like they are apprenticing for skills that will give them a better life.

The benefits of apprenticeships.

I wish we still believed in apprenticeships in America, especially with our educational system being what it is. The painful part is that we miss our chance for apprenticeship during a time in our lives when we can "afford" to earn as little as possible while learning a trade. The apprenticeship system is powerful. Robert Greene talks about the benefits of apprenticeship in his book, *The Mastery*. I suggest that you read this book. As Greene points out, the three steps of apprenticeship are Deep Observation – or the passive mode – and then Skills Acquisition, which is the practice mode. Then there is the Experimentation Phase, which is the active mode.

Think about why apprenticeship makes sense. At 12 or 13, when you don't really "need" money, you could in theory work for free. By the time you're 17 and 18 you could start your own business. We honor the founding fathers and wonder how they did all that they did at an early age. Because they started working when they were 12! They started putting the printing press together at 12 so they understood how everything in the printing press worked by the time they were 17. They weren't focused on high school and going to college. That path wasn't available to a whole lot of people back then. I liken your first deals in real estate to an apprenticeship. You do your first deals for experience. Profit comes with greater experience and knowing what you're doing.

You might say, "But, J., I need an income!" Hey, I get it. Guess what? You are going to need an income tomorrow, too, so the

experience is way more valuable than the amount of money you're trying to earn on your first deal. Here's what I really think... Give me a group of people who are willing to work for free (at least at first) and I can guarantee you that those are the people who will have the right attitude, who are not greedy, who will put themselves out there in a big way and will eventually be able to produce something of value to the marketplace. In turn, this mindset won't just make them wealthy, but it's my bet that they'll be able to do lots of good for other people in the process.

When you tell me that you have to earn an income, what I see is that you're experiencing fear. This fear thing is what you need to use to develop courage, but I understand it. You think, "What am I going to eat? How am I going to be able to pay rent? This and that and the other thing." With this mindset, you'll shortcut the process and settle for, "Just pay my fee." In this mindset, you'll say, "I need money now. Forget what I'm supposed to be learning." This doesn't just happen in the real estate community. I don't care what you're doing in life, you need to keep learning and stop settling. For example, if you take a job, take it to learn the business. Take it to get valuable experience so that you can then go and do something cool with your knowledge.

Say you want to own a fast food restaurant. Why not go to McDonalds and take a job there to learn how they do things? Sure, McDonalds has "great burgers," but it's not only that. Their systems are phenomenal! Wouldn't it then benefit you to work every position? Maybe it's not McDonalds. Maybe it's In-n-Out Burger. They also have terrific systems. What I'm saying is to go somewhere and work every position to learn great systems. And it won't take 20 years of dedicated service to learn it all like it would in a corporate job.

The whole point of business is to improve the quality of life of the customer – solving their problems – but you have to learn how to understand their problems first before you can solve them. Let's go back to McDonalds. We don't go to our favorite McDonalds because we want a place where we can eat healthy food. That's not the problem they are solving. McDonalds solves a different problem. It's the convenience of being served food quickly. If I need to feed my kids something right now and you as a business can help me with that… plus you happen to provide a recreation area that would help me out, well, I'm eating there from time to time and I'm bringing my kids! (Remember I have young kids, so I go to McDonalds sometimes, and it's not for the salad.) Fast food restaurants that want to stay in business understand a parent's mindset. If they keep making burgers and providing recreation, and we keep making kids… ta-da! They'll be successful. They are solving a problem for parents the world over.

Don't like the idea of working for a fast food place? What about Wal-Mart? They have excellent systems. Get hired and work every position. Or look at cruise liners. It's hard for me to take a cruise because I'm so busy watching everything around me that I can't relax. This is especially true at dinner. I watch the orchestration of events and I know in the back of my mind that the wait staff is the tip of the iceberg. (I know.

Maybe I shouldn't use that analogy when talking about a cruise ship. My bad.) There are hundreds of people eating dinner and a lot of workers helping to get the food served. But I know I am only seeing the top part. I'm not seeing what is going on below decks in the kitchen and what it takes to get all that food up to the guests nor all the customization to get that part running right. Everybody has to be speaking the same language, which is interesting because they are all from different countries.

The crazy thing on a cruise ship is that no one person works one job. The person who serves you at dinner could also be the one leading the recreation events on the upper deck. I look around and think, how on earth do they keep this stuff straight? And what about the maintenance people? You never see them, but they are on board. They are there doing their jobs. I am amazed and impressed by those systems that must be in place on that cruise ship. Teach me how to build that type of system and provide value through the system. That would be awesome! You should be excited by learning systems. Then you can build a system that works in your business.

Within that system your team members will each have a role. I pay them to take on the different duties. It's well worth it for me. It means I don't have to do everything. When I say, "There are people for that" I mean that I don't have to do everything. I am the CEO of my company, yes, but that doesn't mean I do everything. It's like cutting one's own fingernails. I don't do that now. There are people for that, and I learned the hard way to accept this fact. I like to share this story at workshops, because it drives my point home.

We can cut our own fingernails and there is nothing wrong with that. I used to do it, too, but I'll let you in on a secret. I happen to enjoy getting my hair and nails done. It's a wonderful experience. My girls told me to do these things, and usually I'll follow their lead. But one day I decided that I could cut my own fingernails. Maybe not. I cut them too close! We have all done this. It hurt! I walked around upset for a couple of days, irritated because my fingernails were cut too close. Every interaction was then tainted with my focus on my fingernail thing. Then I made a Facebook post; it was something like, "How old do I have to be before I actually learn how to properly cut my own fingernails?"

My CFO responded with, "You know, J., there are people for that." Yes, yes. I know. I could have avoided going through all the frustration I did because I was too stubborn to pay someone else to cut my nails. People provide this service. *There are people for that.* My point? Don't think you have to do everything in your business yourself. In fact, it's best to look outward on most things.

It's not about YOU.

As an investor, don't think about "your" single-family home. Think about "their" single-family home or multi-family dwelling. You aren't going to live in the home, are you? Think about how you can make the place better for "them."

We (the team) do this in every deal now. For example, we sat outside of a 182-unit complex one day. We were looking at it, deciding if we wanted it or not as an investment. We wanted to know what "they" need... the people who will be renting this building. Cable! People want cable and they don't want it to look ugly. They may not have the credit to get the cable themselves. What if I solve the problem by negotiating a good business package price on cable and pass the savings on to the renters so they don't have to go through a credit check? That's a bonus! This comes from thinking about what "they" need and not what I want or need.

When looking at a property, ask yourself, "What is the user experience?" The more I know about the uses of a property the more I can help the tenants have a better user experience. An acre of unused land can be turned into a day care center. As a result, because I've ultimately made the lives of the tenants easier, occupancy will be higher and people will rent longer. These are things my team and I think about all the time.

The first step in any deal is to answer, "What do they need?" Not how much money we need. We then do a cost/benefit analysis to figure out costs to do what we need to do with the property to answer the needs question. No matter what type of property, the same question must be asked. What do they need? If it's a commercial property, is it a parking lot? Maybe you'll end up working with your city to help the decision-makers solve problems. If so, you might really have to push your ideas outside the box to think most creatively.

263

To illustrate this point, let me share with you an interesting interaction I had with a participant at an event. One guy told me that he wanted to build a power plant! He had land and wanted to build the plant because that's what was needed in his neck of the woods. He would have to raise capital, build the power plant, extend up and flip it for a really good profit. And that's exactly what he did. Some people might want to own an airport. Okay. In that case, we would have to think, "Who is the airport for?" Maybe people with private jets and pilots. Maybe flight trainers.

What about a jail? Occupancy is always high in jails. Don't laugh, but there is always a waiting list to get in and you don't ever have to worry about evictions. That might be a creative use of vacant land. The point is to ask, "What do 'they' need?" Look for the problems. The bigger the problem, the bigger the solution, the bigger the opportunity, the bigger the profit. As a real estate investor, you have to ask lots and lots of questions to get to the point of providing solutions. I am a real estate investor, which is an ideal business for me. It can be ideal for you, too.

Investing in real estate is IDEAL!

You've heard the word "ideal," but have you ever heard of the acronym IDEAL? It reflects the five components that exist inside real estate that provide lots of advantages to investors! I'll break it down for you...

264

Income – In real estate, you make "income" when you sell your property. I'm sure you've seen on late-night TV where people buy and sell properties in a short period of time. Maybe 60 to 90 days. They buy a property that needs more curb appeal and some fixing up on the inside, spend a little money to get the house looking better, and then they sell at a profit. That profit is an income. When you "fix 'n' flip" like this, you will usually pay taxes higher on the income, otherwise known by your tax guy as "capital gains" or ordinary income. You made a financial gain of capital (money) and, as income, you will pay taxes on it unless you figure out something. There's another form of income that I like a lot. It's called "dividends." To me, this is the better form of income and it's ongoing. What's called "dividends" in the stock market is called "rent" in the world of real estate. In having a tenant pay rent month after month, every 30 days, you're holding and maintaining control of an asset over time, which allows you to use it without selling the asset. It is better for taxes.

Depreciation – One of the best gifts from our tax code, this gives us real estate investors a way to legally deduct a "phantom" expense. In real estate, there is a tremendous amount of depreciation that you can take! If you have a capital expense and you have proof of that expense (i.e., receipts), you get to deduct a certain amount, year after year, for several years on that expense. Different expenses come with different depreciation values. This one excites me to no end. I'll get to the WHY in a little bit.

Equity – Simply, this means that there is more value in a property today than when you purchased it. You hear about "equity" all the time. It could result from a homeowner paying down the principle on the mortgage note. It could be that the loan adjusted down and the property owner now owes less on paper than the house is valued at. This is "amortization" and this is something that happens around traditional home loans. It's not something we have a lot of control over as investors. We do, however, have some control over creating equity situations. Think about short sales for a second. When you buy a short sale property, you're getting it at considerable discount... far less than what the property's value truly is. There is a lot of equity built into the property from the get go. (This is also a form of income.)

Appreciation – This one comes in many forms! You have Found, Forced, Phased, Inflated and Passive appreciation. I don't concern myself with the last two, because I have no control over them. They have to do with what's going on with mortgage regulations and the economy. They have nothing to do with my actions and decisions. I can't affect change in these two areas of appreciation, which I'll explain more about in just a minute, so I stick to the first three forms of appreciation. In short, appreciation is measured in dollars and reflects how much in value a particular asset goes up. Period. That's it. There are many things that can change appreciation and make it go up. You can totally affect this change!

Leverage – To me, this may well be the number-one key to real estate success! When you leverage something, you are using one thing to move another. Think about a large boulder and a few big sticks. To move the boulder you will have to leverage it into the place you want it to be by calling upon other people to help you move it. The tools you are leveraging in this scenario are people and some really sturdy sticks. You are leveraging the people, their skills, their time, their knowledge and some handy tools. (In real estate, the tool is their money.) Maybe someone in the group has a particular understanding of just how to move that boulder. You would then also be leveraging that individual's knowledge. This sort of thing happens all the time in business. In real estate you use leverage all the time and in all forms. Many times it is financial leverage (using other people's money or creating a financial agreement with the seller of a property). In short, leverage means taking a little bit of your own resources and magnifying their power so you can accomplish more. Learning the techniques necessary to make that happen is exactly what I think many of us should be learning from kindergarten through twelfth grade. If we did we would know how to gain new techniques, new understandings and new strategies to increase our time and leverage the talents, skills, time and knowledge of others to help us all get more of our goals accomplished.

Now that you understand what IDEAL means, let's move on to how you can use the IDEAL components to benefit your deal. For this you have to understand what type of investor identity you are dealing with and how to best benefit him/

her. For this, we go now to the **Profit Analysis Quadrant**™ (P.A.Q.), because there are four categories you need to understand when talking to investors who will help you reach your goals in every deal. Each investor will fit into one or more of these quadrants!

Welcome to the P.A.Q.

Where you start out is not where you stay. For example, you might start out as a Wal-Mart shopper, but eventually you can move on to become a Nordstrom shopper. What I'm saying is that when talking to investors you have to understand as much about their world as you can. You can talk to them in a way that makes them understand where they fit into the P.A.Q. Once you understand their investor identity and where they fit in the quadrants, you can figure out how to best serve them. Every investor falls into one or more of the quadrants.

In short, the P.A.Q. is made up of four areas or quadrants. The first is Appreciation (A), the second is Depreciation (D), the third is Amortization (AM) and the fourth is Cash Flow (CF). These are all ways to show potential real estate investors how their money will work and how you will make their money back for them through a deal over time plus returns. Below you will see the P.A.Q. drawn out.

PROFIT ANALYSIS QUADRANT

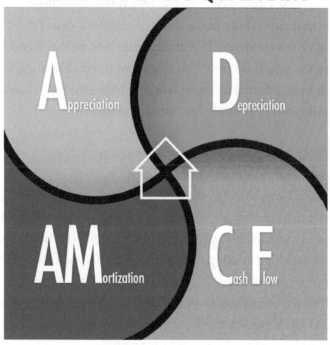

I don't want this to be like a math lesson and I won't go into it fully here. I'll be offering Mastermind Group sessions on this topic and I cover it in my workshops. If you are interested, please drop me a line via my website. Thank you. What I will go over here are the basics so that you have an understanding about the different types of investors and how each quadrant works. I use this quadrant all the time when talking with investors. It's a way that we can figure out where they fit in a deal. (Or if they fit at all.) It allows me to run through different scenarios (different problems I can solve) in the quadrant.

I won't spend much time on the AM Quadrant either, because that's what lenders use, and the lending business in another book entirely. I also won't go too much into cash flow, because that's what this whole book is about, creating cash flow from real estate investments. If you pay attention to the A and D quadrants, you'll do fine. You just have to be able to explain these two quadrants to those who are interested in helping you with your real estate investment goals.

The P.A.Q. is critical to understand for larger deals. As you grow as a real estate investor you truly have to understand the P.A.Q. and how your investors fit into it. Simply, the P.A.Q. is a cooperative arrangement between you and your investors. I believe in cooperative capitalism and that's what the P.A.Q. is! You are gaining the cooperation of others to use their money to buy into larger and larger deals. They will only cooperate with you if they understand how the deal will benefit them. The A and D Quadrants are where you often can, but not always, find most benefit for them and for yourself.

When it comes to the **Appreciation** Quadrant, there are five forms of appreciation and we as investors aren't interested in the last two:

Found – You make your money when you buy (i.e., a short sale).

Forced – You make your money from what you did to make the property worth more money (i.e., a fix 'n' flip).

Phased – You make your money when you add something to the property over time (i.e., adding a day care center or a laundry room).

Inflated – Determined by economic INFLATION, appreciation that occurs in this Quadrant is something you have no control over.

Passive – This form of appreciation can happen randomly due to various reasons over which you have no control. I spend no time on this subject, because I have no control over a geographic area or the fact that the area that was once unpopular is now suddenly hip and everyone wants to live there. However, if that's happening, I will FIND appreciation in properties, I can FORCE appreciation by fixing them up to be what buyers want and I can PHASE appreciation over time by adding amenities the buyers want. I do have control over that.

Why do you as a real estate investor have to understand appreciation and depreciation? To take advantage of tax incentives and to pass tax incentives on to your investors! For example, you don't have to pay back returns on a monthly schedule to investors. You can come up with creative solutions, like no payments for 18 months. First, you have to make sure all of your costs are covered up front. And, believe me, there are costs. This means you shouldn't be making payments to investors until all up-front costs are covered and you're actually into a profit zone. Ideally, you will form an LLC for each property that you purchase. In larger deals, there are legal fees involved. There's an accounting team that will cost you money. You'll want to have your balance sheet audited. Unless you know how to do this you're going to have to hire someone who can. These are all up-front costs that have to be factored in so you can figure out true appreciation.

On the Depreciation side, there are tax deductions that you have to understand. For example, if you are providing energy, food, housing or jobs, you get some pretty nifty tax deductions. In the tax code – and I am not telling you to read the 70,000 pages of tax code (at least it feels like 70,000 pages) – you need to at least know this one line: "All income is taxable unless otherwise described." You need to understand what this statement in the tax code means. Do you have income in a real estate transaction or is this a different type of value?

There are four things that the IRS generally says that you can do to get your tax money back as a refund. The number one thing is to simply provide food. Providing food is a necessary component for living. If you do that, the government has subsidies and has the "ability" to give you your tax money back in tax credits. (That means they can, but you'll have to speak with a tax expert to help you through the application process to receive those credits.) Another thing you can do is to provide energy. You might know that oil and gas is very popular right now and energy is something we all need. Providing energy is something that allows you to get access to lots of the tax credits. You can also choose to provide jobs, which is a lot of fun. You can create a business around an idea, and then you put some structure around it. Next

thing you know, you're providing jobs and opportunities for other individuals, and ta-da! The government gives you tax credits for your efforts. Then there's providing housing. When you provide housing, you also get access to more of the information that's available inside the IRS tax code.

Here's the key... If you choose not to provide one of those four things, what ends up happening is that you PAY for the resources that the people need who actually are providing those four things. The tax code is what is called "revenue neutral," which means for every tax benefit you receive, someone else has to pay for it. If you're not the one receiving the tax benefit, you're probably the one paying for the tax benefit that other people are receiving. Why not be on the winning side of that equation? We get to choose because we live in a great country, where we have the opportunity to choose to be whatever we want to be. Take that option and tax benefits that are rightly yours as a real estate investor who can provide housing!

Knowing some of the tax code can help you!

How can knowing the tax code help you? Think about this... Because of rules in the tax code, my VPO worked it out with the government so that we our property taxes frozen on some of our properties. How can we do that? Legally! We are solving problems. This is true. But we are also receiving tax benefits, because we understand the power of depreciation and how that works when we are rehabbing a building. For

273

example, did you know that you can take a tax depreciation of a residential property over 27.5 years? Yes! For commercial real estate it's 39 years. Because I am not a tax guy, I'll leave you with that bit of information. If I were you, I'd be calling my tax guy and asking him a lot of questions. I'd be reading up on depreciation and how I could be deducting a lot of expenses. That's part of the point of this book, by the way. I want you to WANT to educate yourself beyond my words. Bother to keep learning. Oh, and get yourself a good calculator. You're gonna need one as an investor!

Figuring costs takes math.

You may wonder how we figure out how much everything is going to cost before we start construction in a rehab. It starts with a good property manager who can answer all of your questions. The property manager can give you a spec sheet on what a potential tenant would like in his/her unit and this can then lead to creating a list of construction costs so you have a general idea of the costs in rehabbing a property. I can make a fairly accurate estimation of the costs of any rehab at this point in the Memphis area based on my experience with the other properties I have rehabbed there. That started with input from a good property manager.

Here's the deal… I don't really have to know all the costs that are going into the rehab. I make my offer, contingent upon inspection. For example, if I didn't see something that an inspector sees down the road, and that something is going to cost me a lot of money or just be something I don't

want to deal with, I can withdraw my offer. I can withdraw that offer right up until the time agreed for me to release the contingency. So, my offer stands until I receive an inspection report and if I think things go well, I then hand that report to the construction guy, who really tells me what's up. So remember this: Based upon what you find you can always renegotiate. This is an important point for you to understand. If in the time of escrow you see too many problems and you really don't want to deal with the problems or you feel like you cannot solve the problems, you can say no. You can walk away from the deal. Even after signing the contract you can say, "No, stop, I am not moving forward with this deal!" One of the most useful things I ask for in a transaction is that the inspection period does not begin before the buyer receives all of the documents, and it usually takes nearly every seller about two weeks to get all the papers together.

We get so caught up in the technical goal of acquiring properties that we forget that real estate is a business. If you want information on how to stop being a technician so you can start thinking like an entrepreneur who runs a business, read Michael Gerber's E-Myth. This author also offers books on CD, so there is no reason not to "read" his work. God knows, I "read" all the time while driving or doing other things! (I love audio books.) In short, technicians have a hard time thinking entrepreneurially. As a real estate investor you are going to have to think entrepreneurially. You can't get so caught up in the minutia of the deal that you over-think it and kill it. One of the questions I hear a lot is an example of investors over-thinking things. What's that question? Here it comes...

Which comes first, the offer or the down payment?

I wish I had $10 for every time I've heard this question. So, let's think creatively through the answer, shall we? Let's say you have a teenage daughter. Now let's say you're in your car and you're pulling up to your home from work right now. You see your daughter pacing in your driveway. She looks at you with wide eyes, all serious and dramatic. You jump out of the car and rush to her. "What's the matter, Sweetheart?"

She says, "I simply must have my wedding dress tomorrow. I must have my wedding dress tomorrow!" She is clearly stressed out because she doesn't have her wedding dress. You scratch your head. Myriad thoughts go through your mind. Your daughter is just 13. Why is she stressing about her wedding dress? Things are out of order here. In most states, you have to be older than 13 before you can legally get married. So, you say, "Okay, Honey, hold on. You're 13. You're worried about the wedding dress? Why on earth are you worried about that when you have at least five and possibly 10 years before you're really going to be getting married?"

Your daughter obviously has no need for the wedding dress just yet. So let me ask you this: WHEN does your daughter really need the dress? What is the absolute last possible day and time that she needs that wedding dress? Let's assume she was planning on getting married at 3:00 on this future special day. Ideally, she needs the dress that day. In very real terms, your daughter doesn't need that dress until she is literally getting dressed for her wedding.

Ah, but you're shaking your head, "J., she's going to need to try it on, isn't she?" Yes, she is. And there are other steps, too. Does she even have a location? Or what about the bridesmaids? Who will she choose to be her bridesmaids? Who else will be in the bridal party? And, speaking of the bridal party, shouldn't there be a groom? Who is she marrying anyway? But none of this is the concern right now as your daughter stands in your driveway with a painful expression, telling you she needs her dress and that she needs it tomorrow.

This is what I think about when people ask me when they should place an offer on a piece of property! Then they may ask, "Where's the money going to come from?"

My response is always the same. "Does it matter? When do you absolutely need the money? Do you need it right now… today, the day you place the offer?" The answer, most of the time, is no, you don't. Only in rare circumstances do you need the money the same day you make an offer. Besides, even if you need the money on the same day, you at least have a few hours to go and get it. However, this is usually for auction properties. In auctions, there could be times that you would be able to make a deposit on the property and have up to 48 hours to come up with the rest of the money. In this case, even though you made the offer (a.k.a., your bid) you don't need all of the money right then. Some people won't take the first step in making an offer because they don't have the money YET. Don't be one of them. Go out and place offers on three properties immediately! Then make offers on three more.

277

Making a deal? Think like a programmer!

Today I am a real estate investor, but I was once found joy in computer programming. "But, J., what does that have to do with real estate investing?" More than you think. Stick with me. This is going to sound weird, but I think a lot of people should spend more time learning computer programming. Here's why. To effectively program a computer you can skip no steps. The last step is irrelevant; you don't even need to think about it until all the preceding steps have been perfected or things are at least functional. This viewpoint and experience helped me at the beginning of doing real estate deals, which is something I didn't realize until I saw a video about how programming forces you to compartmentalize your thinking.

Let's talk about this for a minute. When do you actually need the money for a real estate deal? The day you write the contract? No. You don't need it until the day of closing. When do you actually need the contract? Is it the day you meet the seller? Not really, or at least not often, but it depends. What do you really need first? You need a seller to talk to and you need to reach some sort of verbal agreement with him/her. That's step one, and that's the beginning. At this point you are not concerned with doing the paperwork. You aren't to that step yet. You are still on the step that requires you to get out there and talk to people, to find the problems and then to provide solutions. When you get to the paperwork step, it's just going to be a representation of what you have agreed to do for these people and what they've agreed to do for you verbally. I get on the phone all the time and I just repeat what I told the sellers

and buyers I was going to do for them, and then have them repeat what they said they were going to do for me with my attorney present. He makes up the paperwork and sends it to the different parties. Done and done. That's it!

Learning to program a computer taught me to break things down in steps. I can't do step three before doing steps one and two. As a programmer, you think in modules; you have to think in little blocks to be able to make the whole thing work. You also learn to think in very literal terms, because a comma and a period are not the same thing to a computer. They are very different things and they cause a different result. When we use our words in the real world it is the same thing. For example, I could use the word "safe" and everybody who is either reading or listening to this word comes up with something different as a picture in their heads. To some, "safe" is a literal bank safe. Some may think of a bank vault, some think of a floor safe, some think of being safe. Well, what did I really mean by that word? You don't know without further inquiry or investigation, and learning to program a computer teaches you to have the patience to do the inquiry and investigation to find out what the computer really interpreted. Garbage in, garbage out. If you give the computer garbage, that's what you'll get back.

Now let's carry this theory to real estate. I have to be VERY clear in my language to make sure the investor and I are on the same page. Here's an example: If I say that I'll sell you 14% of my equity, which is a different valuation than selling you 14% from the equity of the building. Those two things are completely different; the numbers are totally different! I said "14% OF my equity" vs. "14% FROM the equity." Yes, it's still 14%, but saying it one way means 14% of the whole and saying it the other way is 14% of whatever percent I own. If you are not paying attention that could become a problem. It is simple little words like that I am listening for when talking to sellers, buyers and investors. When I'm negotiating you will hear me ask, "Well, what that means is…" because I want to make sure we are clear. You may also hear me say, "So what you mean is…" because words should be a representation of action.

Sometimes to further clarify, I'll say, "Why did you ask that question?" I will stop in the middle of a negotiation to say something like, "Ask me a question" or "What question would you have if you had one?" Then I'll follow their questions by asking them why they asked THAT question. If you're in a negotiation with me, you could ask any question. It is not the question that's important; it's WHY you asked the question that I want to understand. I am always digging for the why, because that's where the "magic" is. I learned to ask a lot of questions from programming computers. I also learned patience.

As I mentioned earlier, my first computer was a Commodore VIC-20 back when instead of floppy disks we used tape… literally cassettes. It took forever to save the program. Oh, God, that was a process, because you hit SAVE and the tape would have to spin to the right spot and then find a blank spot and then start recording. The tape would just spin and spin

and spin. It took forever! Depending on how long your code was would dictate how many tapes you would need. Later, to install the program, you had to load them in the correct order. Back then, there was not much memory… something like 512K. You can't even play a song with that little amount of memory, but back then it was awesome. Think about that. Today, my iPhone has a ridiculous amount of memory! With this amount of memory I can do a lot of things. I can do calculations at a table to see how I can help solve problems for sellers, buyers and investors. I can do this in California or I can do it across the globe. I can't assume that I can only help people in my country either!

Don't assume anything.

You may think that you can't be a problem-solver in another country or when dealing with people from a culture other than your own. That is a wrong assumption. While the rules may be different the principles remain the same. Here's what I mean… Let's say you are a woman in Saudi Arabia. You want to purchase properties there, but as a woman you feel you have no power or authority to do so. This actually came up in one of my workshops. It's not correct thinking. It should be more about HOW can I, as a woman, invest in real estate in Saudi Arabia? There are women who own businesses and properties there, so obviously it is possible. It is proven. So HOW do you get there? Ask, "As a woman in Saudi Arabia how can I own real estate there?" Then you find the answers. Stop assuming and stop over-thinking. If I had over-thought my deals in

Memphis, I wouldn't have had as much success in real estate as I enjoy now. You think there weren't rules? You think there weren't issues I had to get through? I did these deals by asking lots of questions. To that end, people have questions for me. One I hear a lot is, "Why Memphis?"

Why Memphis?

First, there is a unique distribution system in Memphis. By that I mean there are a lot of interstates the lead in and out of Memphis, which makes it easy to get to other cities from Memphis. There is also the Mississippi River, and five of the six railways are hubbed at Memphis. There is also an airport hub. This is important to understand if you want to invest in Memphis properties, because the person you are likely going to serve in, for example, your apartment complex, is likely going to be a Wal-Mart customer who works in transportation, including FedEx. (When you're in Memphis you can drop a shipment at FedEx till late in the evening and it will still get to your destination the next day!)

A second consideration for investing in Memphis is that there's no income tax. Tennessee is a very pro-business state. The cost of wages is low, and I understand the people of Memphis. I have developed good relationships with the City of Memphis, for example, the mayor and other decision-makers who are trying to make Memphis the best place to live, work, play and lay. These individuals lead me to problem properties and look to me for a solution. From my dealings with the individuals who have the responsibility of finding

282

ways to create clean, safe, affordable housing, the trust that is grown between us and those relationships inevitably lead to other helpful relationships with people I can trust. The circle of influence continues to expand, and it makes me happy to be helping people in Memphis. This is not to say I'm not doing deals in other states and countries. I am. The deals keep getting larger, too, which is exciting for me. This is the life I am creating through my actions and it feels great! That's exactly what I want for you.

Throughout this book I've given you plenty of my reasons for participating in real estate. For you to follow my lead or even take your first steps into the world of real estate investing, you have to dive in. Come on in. The water's fine. Have courage and you can succeed!

STEP TEN:

Be Courageous!

"We must build dikes of courage to hold back the flood of fear." Martin Luther King, Jr.

I have been living boldly for several years, and I wouldn't have it any other way. People ask me all the time how I do it. I love this question! Here's what I ask them in return:

"What would you do if you knew you were guaranteed success?"

That's it. That's my "secret." Life is short. Why not live boldly and act in a manner that will move you forward in your life? Suspend your disbelief and tell yourself that you are guaranteed success. Go for it. Take the first small step toward change in your life. Become a real estate investor. Go out and LOOK at properties you might want to make an offer on. Find one you think shows promise and ask yourself... WHAT

285

WOULD I DO IF I WERE GUARANTEED SUCCESS? Then make a list.

- If I were guaranteed success, I would find and receive the money I require to invest in this house.
- If I were guaranteed success, I would ask the people I know to invest with me.
- If I were guaranteed success, I would fix this house up and rent it out to make cash flow.

Now you create a few "guaranteed success" statements. This will help you get into the right mindset to dive into the real estate investing pool. Once you open your mind to the fact that you are guaranteed success you would actually take your first steps, my question to you is WHY NOT NOW? There is literally nothing physical stopping you from finding houses that need some fixing up and then making an offer. Even here in California I see signs all the time that read FOR SALE BY OWNER. That's a great place to start! Don't over-think the offer, don't make it some big, scary event, and just do it. Just knock on the door and make an offer. Don't fret about making mistakes.

As you know, I've made plenty of mistakes, but I didn't let these "failure events" take away my passion. I didn't let my mistakes take me off my path. Did they impact me? Uh, yes, they did. But they also made me stronger, more knowledgeable and even more passionate about real estate investing than I ever have been. My enthusiasm continues to grow as my goals get bigger and bigger. As I mentioned,

there is nowhere that I can go now that I don't think in terms of real estate. People need a place to live, work, play and lay. That means quite literally everything in life has to do with real estate. Even death has to do with real estate if you think about it. From the time we are born, we function in some type of building that sits on a piece of land. And in the end, we take up a small bit of land with a headstone, or our urn adorns the mantle of a relative's home (i.e., a piece of real estate). We can't get away from real estate, so why not participate in it? And why not do so courageously?

Meet an exemplary new investor…

Want a real-life story on an investor I've been working with… a guy who is new to the pool? He didn't just dip his toe in either. He jumped in like me, cannonball style! He's taking courageous steps in learning how to do what I am doing in real estate now. He gave me permission to share a bit of his tale with you, but I'm changing his name.

This is an investor I work with privately in one-on-one coaching sessions. We'll call him Fred for the sake of this story. Fred shows a great deal of promise as someone who will be very successful in real estate. Why? Because he is courageous enough to believe in himself and he shows a lot of excitement about his plan. In fact, he is sticking to his plan. Fred started with one single-family house and went on to do a couple more deals. His next step might shock you, but he's ready. He is going to make an offer on a large group of properties. Think

I'm going to stop him? No. I applaud his courage! He needed some advice before taking the plunge. In a recent one-on-one, Fred asked me how he could leverage a deal that made the most sense for him and would give him excellent returns.

Fred explained, "I've been talking to a man who has 40 family homes in Springfield, Missouri. They are duplexes and other types of properties. This guy likes using cash flow to buy properties. He is open to selling all of the properties! He wants $2.5 million for all 40. I want to make him a cash offer. I don't have the cash right now, so what can I do?"

I told Fred that there are two challenges. First, we don't see pain with this seller. It's there; we just don't see it. I told Fred to remember that as a real estate investor he is to solve problems. He would have to solve the problem for the seller, which means he would have to assess the actual problem to be fixed. As an investor, you don't buy and sell homes. You solve problems. There is SOMETHING the seller wants. What is it? I would ask him what his equity really is in the properties. He's not after the $2.5M. He wants what he's really after, which might be only $1.5 million.

Second, what does the seller want to do with the money he gets for the properties? If he does nothing with the money, he's looking at paying capital gains of at least $500K. So maybe he has a plan. We need to ask CREATIVE ACQUISITIONS QUESTIONS to solve this man's problems. I need to know what that "something" is that would make him sell. If he doesn't know the answers then the deal's in play. The offer

BECOMES the plan, because Fred is going to lay that plan out by helping the seller figure out the points of pain. If the seller says he has Plan A, Plan B or Plan C, then we are in a different situation. There must be something that is making him think about selling. What is it and what is his plan?

I told Fred that I would get back on the phone with the guy and say, "Hey, [NAME], I have a few questions for you." Ask him about the numbers. Confirm them. Then ask, "What do you owe?" I would ask in a funny way to get to the right answer and to make him relax. He will relax if the questions are infused with humor. Once we know more than we know now, such as that the seller doesn't need ALL the money right now, THEN we can negotiate. For example, if he doesn't have a plan, maybe he will carry some of the paper.

After that, Fred was excited about making a call to the seller. He knew what he was going to say and he had his responses in mind for different possible scenarios. I trust that Fred's gonna do just fine!

Trust is a part of your success in real estate.

You must learn to trust in order to live boldly. "But I've been burned by other people," you say? Okay. That's fine. Me, too. Who hasn't? It doesn't mean you shouldn't trust. Surround yourself with trustworthy individuals who have proven that they live in integrity. Surround yourself with positive individuals… people who share your good attitude and enthusiasm. Be honest with yourself and with others. Stop expecting people to disappoint you. Live by example and you might be surprised by the level of a person who is drawn to you and who will want to help you achieve your vision. Don't make it a selfish vision. Instead make it a SELFLESS vision that puts other people's needs first.

There is an old saying that will help you understand. "If you want to make millions, serve the people on the subway." In my case, I serve families that need clean, safe, affordable housing. (They actually live along the bus route, so I'm serving the people to ride the bus.) In return, I have more than just financial reward. I have spiritual reward, too. Knowing that I am serving these families pushes me to live more and more boldly. I have found my purpose through participating in real estate. What started simply with something I still enjoy doing, which is wholesaling, has grown beyond my wildest expectations. I didn't see some of this new life coming. I didn't know I'd be called upon by city leaders to be a problem solver, but that's what happened. Living boldly and with courage allowed me to say YES to their calls for action.

Hey, I might not be able to draft a contract, but I can hire people whose specialty it is to draft contracts. I might not be able to build a day care center, but I can hire people who know how to build anything I need built. I may not have memorized all the regulations in the tax code, but I can hire accountants and tax professionals who know the rules intimately and who can advise me. I can also educate myself regarding tax laws that govern real estate to make solid decisions. So can you!

290

There are systems of prospecting. Develop a few! I don't think I ever stop prospecting. The leads never stop coming in either! And leads can come from the most unlikely places. For example, while I was in Memphis dealing with the nastiness of getting things worked out with my properties there and talking to the mayor to reach mutually beneficial solutions, an investor I worked with was back here in California. She was at a Starbucks and she started talking to a guy who had massive connections with professional athletes. He happened to work with BCI, an organization that involved basketball camps and educational opportunities.

That conversation lead to an introduction that is still working out well for the charity not just for me but also and most importantly for a bunch of kids! I'll continue to be involved in the camps. It makes sense. I used to play basketball and I love working with kids. I will continue to teach the kids something about basketball AND about financial intelligence. I get them to play the Cashflow game and they love it! Popi and I have used the game as a fundraiser and we've taken it to students in different schools before to teach financial intelligence, so I knew the basketball "campers" would enjoy learning the game. It's great to watch their faces as they start to understand that they can be investors.

These are inner-city kids and I am someone they see as being similar to them. They can see themselves achieve the same thing I have achieved. I get to do this for them because of the troubles I had with Memphis and through working out our issues with the city. I have made and continue to make great new contacts and expand my sphere of influence. For example, I got Bob Weiss, an NBA basketball coach, to come to talk to the kids. I sincerely hope that we'll be doing a lot of basketball clinics for kids and wrapping the Cashflow game into that experience. You can look for our Cashflow Camps for Kids™ soon in a city near you!

I also plan to do a series of wealth-creation system events of all kinds to teach true financial literacy to anyone who is willing to listen and learn. I want people to practice what I teach. In this case it would involve the Cashflow game. The more you play it the more you have a chance to be a successful real estate investor in the real world. You will get the education you need that economics will not teach you. That's something else I hope you got from reading this book!

If you do the right things, your real estate business will grow. It might expand beyond your wildest imagination! You can accomplish the same things I have as an investor. You can do what I did. I developed a system for generating leads, and then I honed that system and added to it. I added online video and podcasts. Each episode takes me about three hours to produce. I write each of the episodes and then produce them. Someone else edits them for me and another person writes the descriptions for me before we put them online. These podcasts (and videos, for that matter) are excellent lead generators. I have a wide audience now, so my leads are even greater. People in Egypt, Africa, the UK, and other countries are listening to me through my podcasts and watching me online. It is all pretty exciting! I have a great passion for what I do.

And that's very important. I advise you to find your passion. Of course, I hope it is in real estate investing. Maybe that's why you're reading this book. What you do with what you learn here is valuable. Do not discount your life.

You can get started and keep going in real estate using little or none of your own money and/or credit. You can use OPM, and you now know that there are things beyond money that other people have to offer that you can leverage. For example, there's OPT (Other People's Time) and OPK (Other People's Knowledge), which comes from your CFO, VPO, CEO, CPA and other professionals with and without letters that follow their names! Frankly, you can use OPE (Other People's Everything)! If there is something you do better than I do, then please… by all means, help me get "it" done better, cheaper, faster, better. Value goes beyond money. If it can be traded, value for value, it's a good thing to consider.

I don't know if you've picked up on the theme of this book, but I couldn't be clearer in my message. You can do whatever you want to do if you believe you can and if you turn off the negative voices in your own head and stop listening to the negative voices coming from those around you. (Even those of your loved ones.) You're going to make plenty of mistakes, so don't be afraid to make them. In fact, it is your next mistake that is the firm stepping stone you need to reach your next level. You will accomplish nothing big alone. You need to build a competent team over time. You can decide to live with integrity, character, purpose and courage. You can determine to surround yourself with honest, trustworthy, action-step people who share your vision. You can allow yourself to let go of old mindsets that hold you back, which will enable you to learn new skills. You can agree to help yourself while helping others. You can decide to participate in real estate and be successful financially and spiritually. You don't need my permission or that of anyone else. The only person holding you back from taking your first steps is you.

So what's it gonna be?

What time is it? I think you know the answer...

CONCLUSION

I sincerely hope that I opened your mind to some of the possibilities and benefits of getting involved in real estate. Did I show you how to fish? (Remember, I'm not just giving you fish; I'm more interested in teaching you how to fish effectively and to keep catching them for life. Then I want you to teach others to fish.)

It was my intent to get your mind to shift away from the traditional path of perceived safety and security of a 9-to-5 job where you have a boss or set of bosses telling you what to do, when to do it and how to do it. If after you have read this you don't start thinking differently about the homes and buildings you pass on the street every day… if I didn't get you to ask yourself what you would do if you were an investor… well, I didn't do a good job of conveying my story. If you don't walk into a drugstore now and really take inventory of what they carry on their shelves, either I didn't get you to open your eyes or you skipped that section. If you don't look at the types of trash cans and where they are placed in the retail centers you visit, I missed my mark with you. By now you should realize that real estate is all around us 24/7 and that you have big clues about the demographics of any location. The information has always been there… right before your very eyes. It's up to you to take this study further, to choose a location and begin your real estate investing adventures. Just be sure to do the homework and research necessary to make the best deals that will bring the most cash flow.

If my story of going from homeless (squatting in my foreclosed home) to real estate investor with hundreds of units of real estate today doesn't show you that you can take the same action steps that I did and get to the same place I am now, I don't know what will get through to you. If on the other hand I drove my message home and you are ready to jump into the pool, then great… The water's fine! Get in here. Swim! Start wholesaling properties. It's one of the best ways to start.

Please chronicle your journey along the way. You can purchase the Diary Component as a companion to this book that has helpful forms and hints that are meant to reduce your stress around taking your first steps. At the time of this writing, we are still working on the Diary Component. If you leave us your contact information, we'll make sure you receive notice just as soon as that component is ready for purchase!

To make it easy, we've created a special page at www. MyCashFlowDiary.com. You'll want to go there and leave

your contact information because we have a gift for you. It's a FREE e-book with very helpful information that you can use immediately. It is the *Investing Made Easier: Networking for Net Wealth*. We will be putting together some very special events around this theme. We will keep you posted!

I want to hear from you. Let me know how your first transactions go. Email me from my website at www. CashflowDiary.com. (But I have to warn you that I don't read really long emails. Keep 'em short, please!) If my team and I decide to use your story – even if it is a story of a mistake or series of mistakes you made – to help educate other new or would-be real estate investors or will help other investors to avoid a misstep in a transaction, we will add it to our Success Stories area on our site. For your convenience, we added a Success Stories form on the site, so you can make your "diary" entries there.

In the companion Diary Component that you can purchase separately (or you are receiving as a part of the Cash Flow Creation Pack™), you will find helpful forms that you can copy and use to assess your own real estate transactions. Questions are included to go along with the steps in this book to help guide you through the process. Use them to change your mindset from closed to wide open. I've even included a section for you to create a Vision Book of sorts. Think of it as your starter book! Then go out and create a Vision Book of your own. Fill it with notes and lists and pictures of the life you want to live. Let real estate investing change your personal picture. In fact, take pictures of your real estate deals and add them to the diary. Make sure we receive copies, too. Send them to me personally through www.CashflowDiary. com. I can't wait to see them! If you're on Instagram, shoot me a pic.

Just in case I didn't cover enough about my adventures in real estate in this book, I gathered a few pages of questions I've received over the past couple of years. These are here as a quick reference for you, giving you just a glimpse of real estate deals in the real world. These come from actual clients I've helped through my one-on-one coaching, Mastermind Group events and LIVE Deal Reviews. May these Q & A's bring you insight!

Q & A WITH J.

Every week I get to help clients by providing solutions to their problems. Maybe it's someone who is a new investor and needs a lot of guidance. It could be a more seasoned investor. Sometimes it's an individual who is taking action by starting his/her own company and needs help walking through the process. There are some very clever people out there. Perhaps you are one of them! I think so. You're reading this book, right?

In my private, one-on-one calls, I answer a lot of questions. It's always amazing just how much ground we can cover together in an hour. I enjoy the heck out of the process, and my clients get the solutions and guidance they need. In my Mastermind Groups I help several people in one sitting. That's like a rapid-fire experience. The participants shoot questions at me pretty fast. It's exhilarating!

I've included several Q & A's to give you a look into my world. I hope this section helps put you on the path to finding

the answers you seek. If not, shoot me an email from my site at www.CashflowDiary.com and we can arrange a time to speak.

C = Client
J = Me!

C: Why real estate vs. other investments? What about a CD (certificate of deposit) vs. real estate?

J: The differences are leaps and bounds. With a CD, you put your own money into a special account at the bank and receive a tiny return at the end of a given period of time. The interest might be 2% or maybe a little more. You'll have to keep your money in that CD for a period of time, which can be six months to several years. The ironic part is that the bank is using your money to lend to people who want to buy real estate. With real estate, you don't have to use your own money or credit. There is no set time limit. You can use debt as leverage, and you use your own effort. You earn a great return if you do things right. (And you can take the money out of a CD to invest in real estate. You'll incur a penalty, but it might be worth it.)

*** *$$* ***

C: I'm confused with my IRA. I want to pull money out now to invest in a property with another investor who has an excellent deal. If I do, I'll take the tax hit. Is this the right thing to do?

J: If you want to get to your goal now, that is the right move. You have to time it right though. Since we are midway through June [at the time of this one-on-one interaction] there's about six months of depreciation left that you can take this year, but that can eliminate the tax debt. If you wait, the IRA grows and taxes grow. Also, property availability is a consideration. Opportunity cost vs. tax cost. That's what you are looking at. I suggest that you do it now. Don't wait. Take action. *It is NOW o'clock!*

*** 𝓢𝓢 ***

C: My plan is to attend more networking events to build my leads list. What else can I do?

J: Networking events are great for you. Printed cards (on yellow thick-stock paper) used as handouts to place on cars work in the beginning. That's what I did. My message was anything I could have fun with. "Increase your income. I did. Find out how!" Or there was, "Like your job? If not, call me now." I started by putting cards on cars. I looked for crowded, close parking. I passed out 600 cards every night and then I walked home. This technique built my network. I started attending networking events and passed out cards at those, too. I also played the Cashflow game with real-life investors and those interested in investing. I listened to audio books at the same time I passed out cards. I was constantly learning! At one point I opened the white pages of the phone book and made cold calls. There ARE leads! The phone book has leads. Passing out cards created leads. As an introvert, this worked well for me. I got an 800# and then talked to people when they called me. I even had some cards that looked like real money to get people's attention. A good message on those is "Turn this into real cash. Call me."

In short, I took ACTION. You could tattoo your message on your forehead. I don't care. At least that would mean you're taking action. I don't suggest that, but what I'm saying is TAKE ACTION. I had too many leads and couldn't keep up at one point! That means I let them go cold. Now I'm far more careful. You need to be careful, too.

*** $$ ***

C: Is there a standard wholesaling fee?

J: No, but when I first got into wholesaling, I took a percentage of the annual cash flow that a property would generate. For example, if the property would generate $200K in a year, my fee was $20K. That is actually too low, so now it's higher. My experience is far greater than when I first got into investing. I understand that the cash flow will bring returns for a lot longer than just the first year!

*** $$ ***

C: What would make the most sense for an elderly investor?

J: That depends on the investor's identity and what he's looking to achieve. That said, I'm working with a guy on a

deal now who is using properties for a tax credit and tax loss strategy. He was purposely losing money in a building to keep it empty. He is also rolling over a CD at low interest to put the funds into a higher-interest loan to me, which makes sense for him. The guy is 80!! From his point of view, it's easier to leave a note to heirs that will make them consistent, long-term cash returns than a piece of property, especially a building. So he is carrying some of the note on one of my deals. Then I split investment buy-in with two other individuals. The first woman is getting 20% and the second investor is getting 16 2/3% return on his money. The deal happened fast. The property was originally valued at $2.5M and within 90 days the value went to $3M! Plus we will occupy it [put renters in place] and create cash flow. The woman investor is in San Diego. She sold land and was cash heavy. She needed a good investment. The other investor was a man in Germany who wanted easy cash flow in the U.S. This deal satisfied the needs of both investors and my needs, too. And it answered the needs of the seller. As you see in this example, each investor identity is different. Each investor has different needs. It's up to me as a real estate investor to understand how best to serve each individual!

*** $$ ***

C: If I attend networking events in California, doesn't that mean I can only do deals in California?

J: NO! You just made an assumption. Assumptions don't move us forward. Just because the people you are networking with

and meeting are in California doesn't mean their properties are or that they wouldn't buy elsewhere. Look at me. My investments are in several states. I use a buy-and-hold strategy.

*** $$ ***

C: A rehabber I know keeps doing $20K deals. He told me that he is upset that you are teaching investment strategies, even some for free with your podcasts! Why do you give so much information away at low or no cost?

J: What I know is valuable. I hear people say they don't have money so they can't invest. I say that if you're going to let something as small as not having money stop you, well, cool. You quit too easy! I was given a gift because of all I have been through. Not everyone can talk from that space, but I can. This upsets some people, but I intend to keep doing what I'm doing for a long time to come. I enjoy sharing my knowledge and educating people in ways they can do what I am doing. When I'm done teaching, you'll know I'm done with real estate. That ain't gonna happen!

*** $$ ***

C: How did you get to the point you are now as an investor?

J: First, I developed an elevator pitch or short message that sums up who I am when I'm at networking events, so I can learn more about who I'm in the room with. "I'm a wholesaler. What that means is, that I buy properties at a discount and sell

properties at a discount. What type of investing do you do?"
Basically, practice your short message and what you do. It's
your networking script.

Also, I had a drawer with a folder so I could keep things more
organized. (There are forms on my website you can use when
you sign up as a Premium Member.) You have to keep things
straight. You need to make notes as to who, what, when and
how, and then talk to the contacts in follow-ups about the
WHY.

*** $\mathscr{S}\mathscr{S}$ ***

C: How did you get the real estate education that got you
started if you didn't have any money?

J: I called people I knew and asked for sponsorship. I read
books, too. Lots of books. I read a lot still. One that was
helpful was Chris Gardener's book, **START WHERE YOU
ARE**. I learned quickly that nobody in my set of friends and
family really believed in me. When I understood that there
wasn't going to be a Calvary showing up to save me and I was
going to have to do this on my own – I was on my own – I
got moving fast. Finally, I got someone who believed in me.
I had ONE WEEK for all my training. I went in with a list of
questions. I vowed to myself that I would do whatever it took
to learn what I came to learn. I knew I could talk to people
for free and started hosting my own Cashflow game events.
I continue to speak to lots of people; I also do podcasts and

radio interviews. These things work well for me now. So do live events. I had to adapt or die!

*** $\mathcal{S}\mathcal{S}$ ***

C: Where did you first hold your Cashflow game events?

J: My wife and I started playing Cashflow games at the clubhouse of our apartment complex or in our house. Eventually we grew to using restaurant space and we negotiated with the restaurant to only pay for the food. It doesn't matter where you start. JUST DO IT. Starbucks is a good place, too. You'll get a lot of interest from playing the game there. I love Starbucks!

*** $\mathcal{S}\mathcal{S}$ ***

C: After I've met new people at networking events, what's the next step?

J: I developed a simple process so I could keep things straight. I kept a folder in a drawer, so it wasn't anything complicated! You can use this system or create something similar, but here is what I do (yes, I still do):

1) Keep blank cards and fill them out with contact information.

2) Next, send these people a *handwritten* note card with a message, "Nice meeting you at [NAME OF THE] event…" Be

sure to add something personal about your interchange with the people from your conversations.

3) Before sealing the envelope, insert a couple of your business cards.

4) MAIL THE CARDS!

This simple thing will generate leads via referrals. It's the "niceness factor." You leverage this over and over again. People will want to cheer you on, work with you and refer you if you treat them with kindness, respect and courtesy. (When's the last time you received a handwritten thank-you note? How did it make you feel?)

C: What type of card?

J: It doesn't matter. Nice picture on the front and blank inside. You are asking for referrals, too. Nicely. "If you have a family or friend who can benefit from my services, please have them call me. I am never too busy to take their call or yours!" This needs to be legibly handwritten.

*** 𝓢𝓢 ***

C: How many hours will I work as a real estate investor?

J: This one makes me chuckle every time someone asks me that question! The simple answer is that you work until you get it done. People want to hear that it will take X number of

calls or X number of contacts before they have a deal. If that's you, go get a toaster. You work until the work is done. It's not an eight-hour day. I had to train myself to be done when the goal was achieved. I had been trained to work eight hours. I was a clock-watcher. Even if it didn't take me eight hours, my brain told me I wasn't done. I'm over that mindset now. Today, I work till the deal is done. Tomorrow another deal will be done. And the day after and the day after... Oh, and I don't really watch clocks anymore either! (Well, sometimes I look at my dollar-value clock. You know... $500 where the number 12 would normally be? I love that clock.)

*** *$$* ***

C: What's a quick example of a property you purchased with none of your own money or credit that brought the best returns?

J: Well, now... Let's take a 62-unit building with a selling price of $800K. If I put $400,000 down (that other investors handed me to put into the deal) and $400,000 was carried by the seller with all the repairs included in that price, that's a good deal. Knowing how to do this type of negotiation comes from experience. The cool thing is that by the time we're done with this particular property it will be worth $1.2 million! BTW, it is 80% occupied at the time of this writing.

308

C: What is a "transactional funder"?

J.: That's a very helpful person to know! When buying a property, you may need a transactional funder, the guy or gal who will let you use his/her money for up to seven days. This person will likely charge you three, four or five points, plus 10% to let you use the money short-term so that you can close on a deal. This is just long enough to sell the property to someone else for a good profit.

*** $$ ***

C: I discovered two challenges internally. As I read all of your materials, watch your videos and listen to your podcasts I see that it's good for me to stick with one track. I want to help people through buy-and-hold strategies. What can I do? [This question came right after this person had attended a networking event.]

J: You've chosen your customer. Now we have to look at the bell curve. We have to look at geography and demographics. In California RIGHT NOW, who has $400K and who has $50K? I mean, do you think more people here in California have which amount?

C: $400K?

J: No. $50K. I am talking about in cash. Maybe it's only $10K. That's okay, too. You do your first deals for experience. Later you do them for profit. It's the fast nickel over the slow dime! Start with a house valued at a $50K or below first, plus a minimum of 15% cash flow. That's why a lot of my deals are not in California. Networking events are really important when looking for properties, no matter what type or range. You were just at a networking event. That means you were in a room with people who have $10K in their bank accounts. Keep that in mind when you go to networking events for investors.

*** $$ ***

C: Have you ever been involved in anything besides real estate outside the corporate sales world? I know you did sales as a W-2 employee, but were there steps before real estate that moved you into doing investing?

J: Yes! I was involved in an MLM because I believed very strongly in the product. It was a special nutritional shake product. I knew the people who started the company and I believed in what they were doing. This was one of my first experiences in business outside of the structured corporate environment and I learned a ton from the man who created the company. I also learned a lot about business and dealing with people. Again, it was a great product. If I don't believe that something works, I cannot get behind it. This product worked! So I got up in front of audiences and talked about it.

I'd ask friends to sit in so they could give me feedback about my presentation. One of those people is Jason, the best man at my wedding. I've known him for more than a decade now. I can always count on him to be a straight shooter with me. We joke. We refer to him as "my normal." It's great to have people in your life like Jason to keep you grounded. (If you're reading this, Jason, I love ya, man!)

*** $$ ***

C: I have a problem in my business. I have hired people off shore who are really holding up my process. I can't move forward when they are dragging their feet, I can't get answers; we have issues in expectations and communication. This is for high-level graphics work. I've paid them well, but I would have to pay people here possibly a lot more for the same work. What do you suggest?

J: Clearly the non-local people haven't worked out even when you pay them what happens to be a good wage for where they are. You have to remember that you're making a decision in all areas of your business. It's always going to be "fast, cheap or good." You can only get two of those three. You tried good and fast. It didn't go well because it really didn't end up being fast. If the people you hire can't deliver on two of the three (fast, cheap or good), you need to reassess. They need to be able to deliver on two, because your time is limited. Here's the problem: It's YOU. Why do you tolerate the behavior? If there are no consequences for their slow action, why would they move quickly for you? Give consequences and keep your word. Stick to the consequences. No excuses. Be clear in your terms. That is your responsibility.

Starting a business takes courage and the right steps.

"I am currently an employee of a corporation. I am a shareholder and the corporation is going to pay me. As an employee whose job needs to be replaced, I'm focusing on what my future organization looks like." Anonymous client who started a business

Starting or growing a business requires a lot of structured planning. I provided guidance to a client who decided to create a special iPhone app to add to a stable of apps he had already created. Until this point, he was an employee who created apps on the side. Now he was expanding his vision by leaps and bounds around the new product. He started an actual business and faced a lot of challenges. This is what we discussed during a series of one-on-one calls.

I'm only going to give you a quick look at what I helped him understand were the steps he would need to take. Once the company was making money he would be investing in real estate, too. His product was a means to an end in a lot of ways. Yes, he wanted to create it, but not for the sake of creating the app alone. If the app was popular with customers, the money he earned from it would give him the ability to invest in large real estate and commercial deals, which is what he wanted to do.

If you are starting a business, and I don't care what type, first you have to create a sales plan for the next five years. This keeps you on track moving forward. Second, you have to get a bead on your expenses. You need to forecast as accurately as you can. In this client's case, he started with his projected costs and subtracted the actual costs of generating his product.

When figuring out costs, it's important to factor in your living expenses. How much is it going to take to cover your personal expenses every month? In this client's case, it was around $4,000. That is a low average here in southern California. You have to know your cost of living in your neck of the woods. Sit down and figure out how much you actually spend each month on the basics. You might be shocked.

In the case of this client who was starting an app development company, there were some issues that came to light as I was talking to him. For example, he was very concerned about taxes. He was told he might end up owing close to $100,000! However, he understood that he had three years to pay the debt off, so he had that part handled. He was relying on an accountant and tax expert to help him with this issue, so we could move on. I'm not a tax guy, so this was a good thing. I don't give tax advice!

The client had to work with different companies in the creation of his product and getting it to the two markets (iPhone and Android). He was running into problems because he had a single point of failure. He needed a backup company to help him with graphics and development. He understood that he needed to do this, and because his current help came from an offshore provider, he wanted to use the services of companies here in the U.S. He would maintain a relationship with the offshore company as a backup. The client was aiming for making his processes more efficient. He would also need a lot of assistance in marketing his product and spreading his message. As he spoke, I realized he was spreading himself thin. The question became what role did he intend to play in his company and how would he work with all the different individuals he would need in order to see his vision come to life.

At this point, the client said he spent a good 80% of his time on testing the apps and on communication. He further stated that if he could find a good tester, he would be happy to relieve himself of that job, too. Then he could spend more of his time building the company and helping to market it. My question to him then became WHY WAIT? Delaying in finding the right individuals who could help him wasn't getting him further in his goals. He agreed to take action immediately and budget for this individual.

Our conversation took many twists and turns. The client would have to hire a bookkeeper and train that person on how to input his particular information into Quick Books, because that's the system he chose to use. He'd have to bring on various individuals to help with everything from development of the new apps to marketing them to continuing to market a few existing apps his group had already created. He was in total growth mode!

One of the most important points of our first call was to get the client to see that where he was spending 80% of his time wasn't where he would be getting 80% of his result. Because he wouldn't be replacing himself right away as the business analyst and tester, he agreed that he'd need to document, document, document everything he did and even digitally record his activities and capture screen shots to use as training aides when he did eventually bring the new person on. That would shorten the learning curve.

I further suggested that he read Michael Gerber's book, *The E Myth*. The book talks about how wearing a lot of hats in one's business will hold the owner back. It talks about establishing systems, too. A business must have good systems in place to run well. We can't do everything on our own, it takes a team to achieve real success and we need systems. Can't argue with that!

In subsequent calls, I learned that even though the client had a good plan and had been moving forward, he was hitting stall points. Some parts of the business worked well and others not so much. One area we discovered that needed help was in the QA (quality assurance) department. He had fallen down on the documentation side of the fence, which inevitably would hurt him. He agreed to fix these issues and to take on an "employer" mindset. He would have to keep his team on point and moving forward. He also had to work on squashing his fears and anxieties about building up his business. He was concerned that he had rushed into things too quickly or that he hadn't made the right choice in moving ahead with expanding his company.

The thing I had to remind him of is that fear isn't going to kill him, and that the fact that he had been really, really busy doing a lot of things to push his company forward toward his goals was a great thing. Notice I didn't say just "good." He was working toward his vision, and that's something to be cheered for! A lot of positive things had happened with this client. He needed to focus on everything he had already moved through. As we moved further into our conversation, he admitted to me that he'd never felt more alive and that he was very happy. He felt more connected spiritually to everything around him. He was happy to be an entrepreneur and business owner. He wouldn't let his fears stop him. Great!

The client was beginning to embrace his role at the helm. He was thinking, innovating and delegating. He was making excellent progress in all areas of his venture. He was serving his customer base that he had defined. He was providing value. He even had his mind to the next steps in his life, which were to buy into a turnkey business with a team and get into the real estate investment game. He agreed with me that as long as these things didn't take from his time in a big way and he built teams to help him to his goals and take on different roles that he could reach all his goals. But he couldn't get there alone. None of us can.

In further coaching sessions, we figured out this man's organizational issues and how to solve them. He then was able to move into a strategic and then tactical path. He was able to understand the value of gathering the best people around him who would share his vision and of seeking good advisors (and then listening to them). He had the old development team work with the new development team to transfer knowledge, and then he was able to get his mind around his marketing objectives and how he was going to move through the steps to get his message out in the best ways. This would also take partnering with other individuals in his field and networking for new opps in apps!

The lesson here is that no matter what business you start, there are logical steps that will move you toward the greatest success. Planning is the first and then thinking through all the areas in your business – from organizational and administrative arms through your strategies and tactical approaches. Everything will affect your marketing approach, so you have to understand your business well… all aspects. That is not to say you have to be involved in all aspects. There are people for that! But you are at the helm and you must decide what your role actually will be. The buck starts and stops with your ability to lead.

WAIT!

You're Not Done Yet...

Please head over the www.MyCashFlowDiary.com and leave us your information. We'll send you periodic updates and notify you when the Diary Component is available for purchase. Plus, we'll send you my complimentary *Investing Made Easier: Networking for Net Wealth e-book!*

Or text the word "journal" to phone number 949.682.3565!